In Search of
My Sober Identity

❖

Stacie H. Cahill

To order additional copies of this book, contact:
Xlibris Corporation
1-888-795-4274
www.Xlibris.com
Orders@Xlibris.com
32367

In Search of
My Sober Identity

CONTENTS

DEDICATION

I would like to dedicate this book to every person suffering from the disease of chemical dependency. I admire each person for having courage and perseverance in order to succeed in the battle for sobriety. I have worked with numerous people who are recovering from this disease, and in doing so, have met some of the most wonderful people that I have ever known.

I owe a very special thank you to my mother for offering her continuous help and support as I spent many long hours preparing and writing this book. She has always been my best friend and I am so very thankful for her! I love you, Mom.

INTRODUCTION

Perhaps you, or persons you love, are struggling with the disease of chemical dependency. I do not think that you have stumbled across this book solely by chance. I choose to believe that there is a reason for everything, and that you are meant to read this book at this point in your lifetime. I would like to encourage you to continue reading while resisting the urge to put the book down for another time. As you begin your quest for self-discovery in sobriety, you will be challenged at times, but it will be well worth all of your efforts. Growing as a sober individual means that you must become accurately in tune with feelings, and that may invoke fear for many of you. In the midst of the disease process, you somehow lost touch with your true identity, and learned to bury feelings that were too painful and overwhelming. You quickly discovered that with chemicals you could forget pain and just become numb to the world, at least for a brief time period. It did not take long for you to understand that you had to have more chemicals in order to maintain a numb state of being. As your disease progressed, you may have even tried to become void of happy feelings. Perhaps you reached a point where a feeling of void was your desire because feeling "nothing" became safer than feeling "something"!

You will learn to accept emotions and will choose to embrace feelings in order to have a content and sober life. Rediscovering yourself as a sober person can be an adventure, and may feel like a roller coaster ride at times; but it is okay, and part of the process of achieving true sobriety. It is normal to have an outpouring of emotion in the early recovery period. You may want to cry and have no idea why you feel the urge to shed tears. You may have brief periods of crying for no apparent reason. You may have periods of laughing and feelings of intense "high". You may experience the giggles out of the blue. You may notice depressed or anxious feelings. There will be times when you will experience intense fear. You may feel irritable or angry for no reason at all.

You must realize that you have numbed your emotions with chemicals for a long period of time, and feelings were stuffed deep within you. In order to develop emotionally and to grow in recovery, these buried emotions must have opportunity to resurface. There will be times when you may want to give up, and you will ache for the numb sensation that you experienced in active addiction. I hope that you will remain committed to the process of discovering your sober person. I want to challenge you to allow the emotions time to flow freely. In order to grow as a sober and healthy person, you must allow yourself to feel again!

Please take time to complete each activity and to answer every question in the book so that you will learn to rediscover yourself as a sober person. Remember that writing your answers in the book is a form of expression, which can be a healthy and therapeutic way in which to express feelings.

CHAPTER 1

WHY MUST I ACKNOWLEDGE MY FEELINGS?

Now that you are sober and working a recovery program, you may be wondering why emotions have so much impact on your recovery. Many people in recovery assume that abstaining from alcohol and drugs is all that is really needed to be well. Others know that a twelve step recovery program is vital for a solid recovery. Many people forget that unresolved and mismanaged emotions can keep an alcoholic or drug addict trapped in the cycle of addiction. Emotions that are not expressed can actually keep you sick.

A person stops growing on an emotional level when he begins abusing chemicals. For example, Michael began to use alcohol regularly at the age of seventeen. By the age of twenty-two he had grown more dependent on alcohol. Due to his alcohol dependency, he was unable to effectively deal with the pressures of growing up. He would bury emotions with chemicals, which would prevent him from working through issues and building healthy relationships. Had Michael chosen not to self medicate with alcohol, he would have been better able to work through identity issues as a sober person. Michael had stopped growing emotionally due to his alcohol use. He simply had lost touch with who he was as a sober person. His first love became the alcohol and he would do anything to protect his chemical. He would lie, cheat, steal, and manipulate in order to maintain his addiction. He put aside his values, morals, healthy relationships, and desires for his drug of choice. Michael could not recognize that working through identity issues and developing healthy relationships are both very important parts of identity. Sure, Michael had accomplished a few things in life. He had a decent job for a while. He got married at twenty-one and had two children. However, the disease of chemical dependency robbed Michael of all the joys in life. He missed out on the rewards of having a happy marriage and healthy relationships with each of his children. His children never had the opportunity to know Michael. He had always put the alcohol before his wife and children. His wife divorced him and moved on with her life. The children had moved away and rarely kept in touch with their father. Tragically, Michael lost his life to Cirrhosis of the liver not long ago. Do you see how chemical dependency robbed Michael of all of his joys in life? Chemical dependency is a progressive and fatal disease. The good news is that it is highly treatable! There is no cure for this disease, which is why you must really put forth effort in order to achieve long-term sobriety. Dealing with emotions is just one important aspect of recovery. As sober individuals, we must learn to be ourselves again. Being ourselves again requires us to listen to our emotions and learn to effectively cope. It is truly a shame that Michael did not have the chance to find his sober person and to grow in a healthy manner. I do hope that you will choose the higher road by making a commitment to become more in tune with your emotions.

Now, I would like for you to focus on the time period in which you first began to use chemicals. Describe any feelings associated with use._____

_____

_____

_____

_____

Do you think that your emotional health was stunted by the introduction of drugs or alcohol into your life? Describe any emotions that were stuffed or buried._____

_____

_____

_____

_____

_____

_____

_____

_____

_____

_____

_____

Can you identify any unhealthy relationships during the aforementioned time period?_____

_____

_____

_____

_____

_____

_____

As we go through life, we will experience the entire gamut of emotions. Emotions are simply energy, or a way of expressing oneself. If we choose not to address emotions, they will not simply just go away. Alcoholics and addicts are sometimes able to temporarily suppress emotion with chemicals. I have heard several chemically dependent persons describe a feeling of numbness as" nirvana", or a place that meets all of their desires. The only time they feel peace is when they are not feeling anything at all. Although burying emotion may cause an addict to feel better at the time, the emotions are actually boiling beneath the surface and are ready to erupt at any moment. Emotions that are buried continue to make the alcoholic and addict sick. Suppression of emotion hinders healthy emotional growth and development. As drugs and alcohol are eliminated from the body, the addict and alcoholic are left with an overwhelming sense of emotion, and many have no idea how to cope with feelings. Oftentimes, additional chemicals are ingested as an attempt to dull emotion once again. The numbing sensation that is desired is short lived and damaging to both mind and body.

In early sobriety it is common to desire a numb feeling once again just like the feeling desired during using days. Many people are left wondering why abstaining from chemicals is not enough to experience a happy and sober lifestyle. Those in recovery must recognize the need for healthy expression through acknowledging and dealing with emotion. It is important to live fully and to rediscover sober self and identity. You will have times of happiness, joy, sadness, and hurt. You will feel angry and fearful at times. You may experience sorrow, excitement, and guilt. Other types of emotions may include: boredom, jealousy, shame, thankfulness, stubbornness, bravery, resentment, hostility, curiosity, enthusiasm, laughter, thoughtfulness, surprise, love, disgust, interest and desire. Although it is not always easy to cope with certain emotions, we must allow these feelings to naturally occur. Remember that it is common to want to escape the emotion. Resist the urge to flee and feel the emotion anyway! Relapse is common in the disease of chemical dependency. The following factors contribute to relapse: not being involved enough with 12 step support meetings, lack of sponsor support, choosing to be around dangerous places or people where chemicals are readily available, and emotional death or simply an absence of emotions.

I have chosen to focus on emotions and self-awareness in this book, not because everything else is of little value, but because neglecting emotions directly affects all of the other important recovery essentials. Inability to deal with emotions will keep you sick in the cycle of addiction and will stunt emotional growth.It is of prime importance that a person in recovery spend time with other alcoholics and addicts in recovery. Working the 12 steps serves as a positive tool in understanding addiction. Sponsor support is vital as you begin to work through emotion.You must disclose your innermost thoughts to another person who understands where you have been and can understand how you are feeling.

To better understand feeling and emotion you must ACT. Recognizing emotion without taking a positive action is useless. You will not grow as a sober person if you neglect to take positive action in dealing with your emotions.

Acknowledge each feeling as it occurs.
Cope with every emotion in a healthy manner.
Think positive thoughts.

Describe any emotions that you are feeling at this very moment._____
_____
_____
_____
_____
_____
_____
_____
_____
_____
_____
_____

Conduct a quick assessment of your emotions today. Please fill in each answer, as it is important for recognizing and assessing your feelings. Please remember that writing your answers in this book will serve as a therapeutic means in which to better understand yourself.

1. Do you have any hidden feelings of guilt or shame? What are they?_____
_____
_____
_____
_____
_____
_____
_____
_____
_____
_____
_____

2. What is your most embarrassing moment? Describe how you felt during the occurrence._____
_____

Are you currently jealous of anyone? Write about these feelings. _____
_____

_____

_____

_____

_____

_____

_____

_____

_____

4.What makes you happy?_____

_____

_____

_____

_____

_____

_____

5. What are you most passionate about in life?_____

_____

_____

_____

_____

_____

_____

6. Are you in love? Describe the feelings associated with being in love._____

_____

_____

_____

_____

7. When do you feel most excited?_____

_____

_____

8.When do you feel most at peace?

9. Are you feeling any anger today? Describe those feelings.

10. Describe how you feel when you are bored. What do you do when feeling bored?

Okay, now that you have completed all ten of the questions, can you say that you found them easy to answer, or were they more of a challenge? Please understand that it may be difficult to answer the questions after habitually numbing your emotions with chemicals.

Now that you have chosen to live a sober lifestyle and have expressed a strong desire to better understand yourself, you must be patient. It may take time to understand how you really feel about certain topics and to know how to better cope with each emotion.

It will be important to ACT when faced with emotion. During using days many people RUN.

React instead of act.

Unravel and respond in an unhealthy fashion.

Numb feelings with chemicals or addictive behavior.

When people choose to run instead of taking positive action to cope with emotions, feelings only intensify, and the need to cover them with some unhealthy behavior such as drinking or drugging, often result again and again. Unhealthy reactions may include the following: acting angry in a volatile fashion, stuffing emotions and sulking, extreme irritability, anxiety, depression, sickness as a result of decreased immune function and stress, drinking and drugging, overeating, and festering resentments. As you can see, it is extremely important to ACT when emotions arise. There are numerous positive actions that may be utilized when faced with certain emotions. Anger management strategies are important. It is important to learn new ways to cope with stress in your life. You must know how to handle guilt and shame. Taking care of your body with exercise and diet is an important component of recovery and emotional management. Building positive relationships is a necessary part of emotional development. Learning to face life through positive thinking is another important aspect of recovery. We will cover each positive action in detail in this book. Please remember that it is okay to feel like you would rather run when troubling emotions surface, as this too, is only a feeling. You cannot deny feelings. They are a part of who you are and how you develop as a person. It is important to acknowledge each feeling. You can, however, choose to ACT instead of RUNNING! You have chosen to live today as a sober person. This is a choice. You must choose to ACT when dealing with emotions as well.

Describe a past situation in which you chose to RUN rather than ACT? How did you react or unravel? Did you numb the feelings with chemicals or some other addictive behavior? _____

_____

_____

_____

_____

Are you currently faced with any situations from which you are running? Describe.

_____

_____

_____

_____

_____

_____

_____

_____

_____

_____

Why might it be in your best interest to ACT in these situations?_____

_____

_____

_____

_____

_____

_____

_____

_____

_____

_____

_____

Do not forget to concentrate on having positive thoughts. The power of positive thinking in recovery is absolutely amazing. Dwelling strictly on the negative and running from emotions can be incredibly dangerous. You must learn to accept your own emotions and to make the best of every situation. If you have an event occur in your life that you are unhappy with, you must address the situation and attempt to make positive changes.

Joy was feeling frustrated and upset because her budget would not allow her to purchase a new automobile. She was in desperate need of newer transportation, as her car had seen it's last days. She had saved money over the last 12 months, as she anticipated that her vehicle would not last another year. She had sacrificed new clothes and dinner out with friends in order to save enough money for the new car. She worked overtime whenever she could and would save every penny that she could save. She had her eye on a new Jeep Cherokee. She did not meet her goal and did not raise enough funds for a down payment on a new car. She simply did not figure into the budget the cost of a new air conditioning unit and her daughter's ballet lessons. She also had to purchase a new washing machine after her washer quit working the previous month. She calculated the cost of the new jeep and quickly discovered that she would not be able to drive a new jeep. She felt aggravated and short changed. She then decided to improvise and buy an older jeep Cherokee. The car had more miles than she had desired, and it surely had a few dents and scratches. She felt disappointed that she was unable to reach her initial goal, yet she was able to think positive thoughts despite her frustration. She thought about other individuals who could not afford any transportation and was thankful that her daughter had the opportunity to take ballet classes. She reflected on her childhood and remembered how her grandmother's house did not have air conditioning at all. The memories were so vivid, that she could recall the sultry heat and could almost feel the perspiration on her nose. She closed her eyes that night and counted her blessings instead of focusing on what she did not have.

What positive thoughts are you having today?_____

_____

_____

_____

_____

_____

_____

_____

_____

_____

Can you describe a time when you were able to focus on positive thoughts despite feeling disappointed or not being able to meet a specific goal?_____

_____

_____

_____

_____

_____

_____

_____

_____

_____

CHAPTER 2

WHO AM I?

Working through identity issues may sound like a huge task. At times it can be, but it is well worth every effort. As you go through life you will experience identity crises. From a very early age, you are already discovering your surroundings and the people inside your world. As a small child, I am sure that you had preferences for certain types of food, favorite toys, and for specific caregivers. Children are in search of their identities. Many younger siblings will model behaviors that they see their older sisters or brothers doing. People at all ages have to try out different personas in order to find who they are. As each of you aged and developed other interests, new identity issues emerged in your lives. You may have enjoyed sports, or maybe you did not care for sports at all. You liked certain types of music and television shows. You probably could not tolerate other types of music. There may have been times when you sort of evolved into someone that you did not even recognize, just to fit in for a moment or two. This is all a normal part of the identity process. I can remember peer pressure quite well. I believed that I had to dress a certain way to be popular in high school. I must admit that my high top red Reeboks were not comfortable, but I suffered anyway.

Describe a time when you did something that you did not necessarily want to do in order to fit in with the crowd._____

_____

_____

_____

_____

_____

_____

_____

_____

_____

_____

Identify your favorite childhood toys. _____
_____
_____
_____
_____
_____
_____

As a child, who were some of your favorite people? _____
_____
_____
_____
_____
_____
_____

As a child, what were your favorite foods? _____
_____
_____
_____
_____
_____
_____

Did you have a favorite sport or pastime? Describe. _____
_____
_____
_____
_____
_____
_____
_____

List favorite television shows or movies you enjoyed during childhood. _____
_____
_____

_____

Describe a favorite childhood activity._____

_____

Answering the questions listed above is an important part of the healing process and will help one in search for sober identity. Sometimes childhood interests offer a glimpse into the soul and provide insight regarding the person you have hidden and the person that you strive to be. After you chose to give up part of your life for the lifestyle of addiction, you simply lost touch with the inner child and your true person. Take a moment and reflect on your answers to the questions concerning childhood interests.

Have you abandoned any of your interests or lost track of the special people in your life?_____

_____

Did you identify any childhood activities that you may want to participate in as an adult? Describe._____

_____

There are two components of the personality which all chemically dependent persons must battle. "The Sober Self vs. The Addict" can be a challenge at times. The Sober Self consists of characteristics and traits that make you who you are. What are your likes and interests? A sober person must be truthful in every situation and in tune with emotions. A person operating in this mode recognizes that it is okay not to feel happy all of the time. He understands that he will feel angry and sad at times. He appreciates that it is vital to deal with the emotions and to resist any urge to bottle feelings because it feels "safer". A sober person will not lie or manipulate others to get what he wants in life. A sober person strives to develop healthy relationships in which there is always mutual respect. A sober person wants to be loved and wants to give love in return. Early in recovery it will take time to reconnect and discover your sober person. Please keep in mind that you have given up many aspects of your life and traded them for drugs and alcohol. It took time for you to cross the threshold of chemical dependency and will take time to rediscover your sober identity. You must be patient as you begin the adventure to search for your sober self. Sometimes feelings may seem overwhelming and you may feel confused or discouraged. We will discuss helpful strategies and effective methods in which to better handle such emotions in following chapters.

A person operating in The Addict Mode will lie, cheat, and steal in order to protect his chemical. He will manipulate others and will become entangled only in unhealthy relationships. He will stuff feelings by numbing out with chemicals, which will cause him to be extremely irritable and unpleasant at times. He feels unlovable and loves his chemical above everything else in life. The addict is usually the exact opposite of a person's true self. The addict is extremely selfish and will sacrifice anything and will lose everything in order to protect his drug of choice. A person operating in addict mode oftentimes has very loose morals and almost always abandons values as the disease of chemical dependency assumes complete control over his life.

Jamie was once a respected and honest father of three. He was married for eighteen years and maintained a solid income for his wife and family. His wife always knew what time he would arrive home from work, and she appreciated all of the help that he provided around the house. Overall, Jamie and his wife enjoyed a happy marriage and shared a deep love and admiration for one another. The kids could rely on their father to be there for them whenever they needed him. He was a devout leader in the church and even served as a deacon. He always made time for others, as well as for himself, and enjoyed his favorite pastimes. He played softball twice a week on a league at church. He was a well rounded and balanced individual until alcohol devoured every aspect of his life. Alcohol robbed him of absolutely everything! He began to secretly drink alcohol as a form of stress reduction. He enjoyed the feeling that he got from the alcohol. He gradually added more alcohol and crossed the thin line of chemical dependency. Eventually, his family caught on to his secret, and everything began to unravel. He tried to hide his drinking from others. He did everything in order to protect his alcohol. He resorted to lying to his wife about his usage, and began cheating his family by robbing them of financial stability. They could no longer trust him, and his morals were no longer his own. He had evolved into a person unrecognized by anyone. His children no longer had peace of mind and they all suffered emotionally as they watched their father disappear. Jamie missed work and suffered major consequences regarding his employment. His once secure employment did not seem so certain anymore. It is so sad to see the devastation the disease of addiction can cause to any person. Addiction does not discriminate and often attacks the finest individuals.

Describe your addict personality.

_____

_____

_____

_____

_____

_____

_____

_____

Did you ever lie, cheat, or steal in order to protect your chemical?

_____

_____

_____

_____

_____

_____

_____

_____

_____

_____

_____

Let us view the search for your sober self as an adventure. It really can be exciting to learn about yourself. Can you think of a time when you established a relationship with a significant other in your life? Do you remember how much fun it was to learn all about that person? It was invigorating to discover their likes and dislikes. It was probably equally fun for them to learn about you! This process of understanding who you are can produce similar feelings of excitement as you rediscover your own identity.

What are your interests? Who are you? Please take time to think about each question before answering. Many people will find the questions difficult. You may not have an answer for every question, as the process of working through identity is new for you at this moment. This is very normal, and you may need to come back to certain questions as time elapses and you gain a solid understanding of the real you!

Write about your favorite type of music. _____

_____

_____

_____

_____

Do you have a best friend? _____

_____

_____

Describe two people you most admire. _____

_____

_____

_____

What is your greatest accomplishment? _____

_____

_____

_____

_____

_____

Do you have a special talent?_____

_____

_____

_____

_____

What are your most important values?_____

_____

_____

_____

_____

_____

What are your favorite foods?_____

_____

_____

_____

_____

_____

What are your favorite television shows?_____

_____

_____

_____

_____

Do you have a favorite movie?_____

_____

_____

Do you have a favorite color?_____
Write about your favorite memory._____

_____

_____

_____

_____

_____

_____

_____

_____

_____

_____

Do you have a favorite book or magazine?_____

_____

_____

What is your greatest weakness?_____

_____

_____

_____

List your character strengths._____

_____

_____

_____

_____

_____

_____

What is your greatest fear?_____

_____

_____

_____

_____

_____

What do you most enjoy about having a sober lifestyle?_____

_____

_____

_____

_____

_____

_____

What are your favorite pastimes or hobbies?_____
_____
_____
_____
_____
_____

Do you have a favorite restaurant?_____
_____
_____

Write about the day in which you made the decision to get sober. What do you
remember?_____
_____
_____
_____
_____
_____
_____
_____
_____
_____
_____
_____
_____
_____

When is the last time you cried? Describe the situation._____
_____
_____
_____
_____
_____
_____

What is your favorite season?_____
_____
_____

Do you have a favorite holiday?_____
_____
_____
_____

Where is your favorite vacation destination?_____
_____
_____
_____

Do you have any annoying habits?_____
_____
_____
_____

Do you have any important sober supports in your life{sponsor, sober friends, or twelve
step fellowship}? How are they helpful to you? _____
_____
_____
_____
_____
_____
_____
_____
_____

What is your best physical feature?_____
_____
_____

Do you have a favorite animal?_____
_____

Name at least one new activity that you would like to explore._____
_____

What would you do with a million dollars?_____
_____
_____

_____

_____

_____

_____

_____

_____

Describe any dangerous people, places, or things. In other words, discuss anything that may threaten your sobriety. Are you taking precautions to avoid the dangers?

_____

_____

_____

_____

_____

_____

_____

_____

_____

_____

How do you feel after answering questions that reflect your likes, values, and personality? Did you learn anything about yourself? After spending so much time immersed in drugs or alcohol, you lost an important part of yourself. Alcohol and drugs became your first love. Everything else in your life became second place to your drug of choice. Now it is time to get back the part of you that is lost. It is time to celebrate who you are!

Let us explore who you are a bit further. What type of personality do you possess? Do you have a strong sense of humor? Do you have a hot temperament? I think of a beautiful rainbow when I try to understand the concept of personality. There are so many different personalities in the world today. All of these unique personalities blend together beautifully as the colors of a rainbow. Think for a moment how dull life would be if everyone had the same personality. We would all be so bored, and there would never be any mystery or excitement in our interactions with others. I am thrilled that we are each entitled to our own set of values, beliefs, characteristics, and behaviors.

Let us explore something I refer to as The Rainbow Personality Chart. Each color of the rainbow represents a specific personality type. As you read about each personality type, most of you will see yourself as primarily one color. Some of you may identify with more than one color, which is okay, too.

A CHERRY RED PERSONALITY exhibits many of the following traits: This person is very passionate for life and tends to practice all or nothing thinking. If he falls in love, he gives 110% to his partner and to the relationship. This person will choose either to invest nothing or everything in an activity or person. He is often hot tempered and can be easily angered. He is usually a very deep and loyal person who will be a friend for life. This person copes with sudden emergencies well. A Cherry Red Personality has high energy and is an excellent problem-solver. He is usually extremely independent and bold.

THE TANGERINE ORANGE PERSONALITY exhibits many of the following traits: This person is usually lots of fun. He enjoys laughter and tends to look for humor in things. He has a contagious laugh that attracts the attention of many. However, he does sometimes mask painful feelings with humor, which can be a pitfall. He is often referred to by others as "the life of the party". He exudes an aura of fun and excitement. He does, at times, have difficulty accepting responsibility for difficult tasks. He can be unorganized with projects or tasks. This person usually has a wonderful imagination and can be very creative. He is sometimes artistic and has a love for nature. He is often open-minded and is willing to at least hear another's viewpoint. This individual tends to be optimistic, and he almost always sees the cup as half full.

A SUNSHINE YELLOW PERSONALITY exhibits many of the following traits. This person is happy natured and full of compassion for others. He can usually put a smile on the face of someone who is feeling blue. He is an excellent listener and a wonderful friend. He makes every attempt to understand you and will help you at all costs. He sometimes becomes over involved with others and runs the risk of becoming codependent. Sometimes this person struggles with self care, due to his burning desire to help others. In some cases, others may take advantage of this person's deep compassion. This person is usually very spiritual. He is trustworthy and will always keep a secret. Sometimes he has trouble showing any sad emotions because he does not want others to feel sorry for him.

THE EMERALD GREEN PERSONALITY exhibits many of the following traits: This person is always willing to try new things. He enjoys change and adventure. This person is a thrill seeking person who is spontaneous and gets bored with routine. He often has trouble with planning and long-range goal setting. This person is strong and often has great physical and emotional strength. He is assertive and can voice opinions well. The Emerald Green Personality is a leader and does not follow others. People look to this individual for help when they are faced with tough situations. This person often has difficulty with money management and is quick to impulsively spend any extra cash.

A SERENE BLUE PERONALITY exhibits many of the following traits: This person is a calm person who is usually at peace with his life. This person tends to be reserved and introverted. The Serene Blue Personality is most comfortable alone or in very small groups. This person is usually a deep thinker. He may appear guarded at times and will study people and things before becoming involved. Others often refer to this person as being shy or backward. He is cynical, and untrusting at times. He does tend to be a perfectionist and does not tolerate disorganization. This person tends to be clean and extremely neat. He manages time well and is super-responsible. He is a wonderful planner. Employers and coworkers often appoint this person to plan projects and to complete specific tasks.

AN INDIGO SPLASH PERSONALITY exhibits many of the following traits: This person is extremely extroverted and loves to socialize with others. This is a people person with excellent communication skills. The Indigo Splash Personality may enjoy being the center of attention. This person is often described as being bubbly in social interactions. He knows no stranger and will strike up a conversation with anyone. This is a very emotional person who is very expressive, both verbally and through nonverbal behavior. He is quick to shed a tear and is not bashful about laughing out loud. Others say he talks a lot. This person tends to have a very healthy self-esteem and a strong love for others. He often has quick wit and enjoys humor. This person is confident with self and is often a high achiever. He does tend to be a worrier, and often is an anxious personality.

THE DRIVEN VIOLET PERSONALITY exhibits many of the following traits: This person is a natural born leader and is often very successful in life. He tends to be more serious and is driven. The Driven Violet Personality does not give up easily and will persevere with most anything he attempts. This person is usually very intelligent and has a strong desire to learn. He is always starting new projects and becoming involved with the community in some fashion. He has a great sense of direction. He is task oriented and motivated for life. This person does struggle with flexibility and can be bossy at times. He likes to do things his own way and may have difficulty working with a team. This individual is accomplished and tends to be very competitive. He is always striving to be number one, and often he is.

Have you decided which color your personality represents? Are you a combination of colors? Your own personality is unique and makes you special. Answer the following questions in order to better understand your personality type. Just place a check mark next to the statements that apply to you.

CHERRY RED PERSONALITY

1. I sometimes get angry easily.
2. Many people say that I am bold in my endeavors.
3. I am extremely passionate and intense.
4. I am independent and prefer to complete a task alone.
5. If I am hurt by you, I may detach and give up on our relationship.
6. When I fall in love, I invest my heart and soul into the relationship.

7. I am a person who handles crises and emergencies well.
8. I am a problem solver in most situations and seek to find the solution.
9. People often say that I am hot tempered.
10. I am loyal to friends and nourish relationships in order to keep them for life.

HOW MANY QUESTIONS DID YOU CHECK IN THE CHERRY RED CATEGORY?
_____

TANGERINE ORANGE PERSONALITY

1. I tend to find humor in the small things.
2. I laugh a lot, and have an excellent sense of humor.
3. I have difficulty being responsible for certain tasks.
4. I tend to be unorganized.
5. Other people say I am fun and think of me as the life of the party!
6. I am very creative.
7. I am easy to reason with and will try to understand the viewpoints of others, even when I do not agree.
8. I have an amazing imagination and enjoy activities that allow me to use my imagination.
9. I am a positive person and almost never view the cup as being half empty.
10. I love excitement!

HOW MANY QUESTIONS DID YOU CHECK IN THE TANGERINE ORANGE CATEGORY_____

SUNNY YELLOW PERSONALITY

1. I am compassionate and care deeply for others.
2. I tend to neglect my own needs due to helping others with their needs.
3. Sometimes others take advantage of me.
4. I am exceptionally warm and friendly.
5. Others view me as their best friend.
6. I am a great listener and I truly care about every issue my friend is facing.
7. I am very spiritual!
8. I smile a lot and am mostly a pretty happy person!
9. I hesitate to express sorrow or unpleasant emotions due to causing those around me to have a feeling of sadness.
10. My friends talk to me because they know that I will always keep their secrets.

HOW MANY QUESTIONS DID YOU CHECK IN THE SUNSHINE YELLOW CATEGORY?_____

EMERALD GREEN PERSONALITY

1. I love amusement parks and other thrill attractions.
2. I am very spontaneous and usually do not like to make plans.
3. I exhibit both physical and emotional strength.
4. Other people ask me for help when they are faced with difficult circumstances.
5. I get bored with routine and try to keep things exciting!
6. I have difficulty managing money and sometimes buy items on impulse.
7. I am a leader and always voice my opinion well.
8. I am almost always assertive.
9. I have trouble with long range planning and goal setting.
10. I am a thrill seeker!

HOW MANY QUESTIONS DID YOU CHECK IN THE EMERALD GREEN CATEGORY?

_____

SERENE BLUE PERSONALITY

1. I am introverted in many ways and am not comfortable in large groups of people.
2. I am very intelligent and I am a deep thinker.
3. I am very neat and organized.
4. I tend to be a perfectionist with most things in life.
5. I am cynical and untrusting in many situations.
6. I take my time getting to know people.
7. Others view me as guarded at times.
8. I am especially good at being calm and content with life.
9. I am extremely responsible and others can always count on me!
10. My employer and coworkers encourage me to plan projects and to complete tasks at work.

HOW MANY QUESTIONS DID YOU CHECK IN THE SERENE BLUE CATEGORY?

_____

INDIGO SPLASH PERSONALITY

1. I tend to talk a lot.
2. I am extremely social and often enjoy being in the center of attention.
3. I worry too much, even over small things.
4. I communicate well and will talk to anyone.
5. Others say that I am bubbly and communicate well.

6. I have an extremely positive self-esteem and am a high achiever.
7. I am very emotional and feel comfortable expressing my emotions, both verbally and nonverbally.
8. I enjoy humor and have quick wit.
9. I have an exceptionally strong love for other people.
10. I am an extremely confident person.

HOW MANY QUESTIONS DID YOU CHECK IN THE INDIGO SPLASH CATEGORY?

DRIVEN VIOLET PERSONALITY

1. I am very intelligent and I have a strong desire to learn.
2. I am always driven and will persevere in every endeavor.
3. I am a very competitive person.
4. I tend to be bossy in certain situations.
5. I am rather serious and seldom have time for fun.
6. I am a natural born leader, and I am very successful.
7. I have difficulty working with a team because I would rather do things my own way.
8. I have difficulty with being flexible.
9. I am always getting involved with some new community project.
10. I do not procrastinate!

HOW MANY QUESTIONS DID YOU CHECK IN THE DRIVEN VIOLET PERSONALITY CATEGORY?_____

In which category did you have the most checks? Remember that most everyone will have at least one check in every category. You will most likely have more checks in one or two categories. The category in which you have the most checks best describes your personality type.

Which personality type best describes you? Are you a combination of personality types? Describe._____

_____

_____

_____

_____

_____

_____

_____

_____

Are you satisfied with your personality type?_____
_____
_____
_____

Are there any characteristics concerning your personality type that you may want to
change? _____
_____
_____
_____
_____
_____
_____

Which characteristics do you admire about your specific personality type?_____
_____
_____
_____
_____
_____
_____

Personality truly is a blend of color and individuality. Every person has his own unique blend of personality traits, which makes that individual beautiful. This is part of what makes each person so special. Personality is not set in stone and does tend to change as one matures and grows. If you are dissatisfied with any aspect of your own personality, you can work on the area for positive change. For example, if you procrastinate and do not like this trait about yourself, you can strive to achieve deadlines. The first step is to identify the procrastination, and then to create an action plan. First, ask yourself why you procrastinate. Is it fear of failure? Is it a lazy streak in your personality, or do you suffer from low self-esteem and lack confidence to take on new tasks? If you lack confidence, you may need to get help with self esteem issues. You can consult a private therapist who will help you identify and build a healthy self esteem. Perhaps you would benefit from a local support group in the area. You may just need to make a personal commitment to get busy and to let the laziness die. It is not easy to change a troublesome aspect of your personality, but it is attainable with a renewed commitment from you! You must make positive changes and act. Without positive actions, change will not occur. You cannot do the same things and expect different results. Do not resign yourself to the fact that an unpleasant personality trait is just a part of who you are. You are the person you want to be, and this is part of what makes you special!

Is there an aspect of your own personality that you desire to change? Describe.

_____

_____

_____

How will you make a positive change? List action steps._____

_____

_____

_____

_____

_____

_____

Do you feel that you may need to consult a private therapist or a local support group
in order to successfully make the change? If so, list names and numbers of agencies of
individual therapists. You will need to use the phone book, or you may find numbers
o n l i n e ._____

_____

_____

_____

_____

_____

_____

_____

_____

_____

_____

CHAPTER 3

MUST I BE HAPPY ALL OF THE TIME?

You may be reading this book and have an inclination that you must be happy all of the time in order to be sober. I suspect you may feel overwhelmed wondering how in the world you will attain perfect peace and happiness in sobriety. You are human, and as a sober individual you will experience many different emotions. Some of the emotions will be feelings of unhappiness at times. It is impossible to be completely happy every minute of every day. You will have some days where it is tough to find happiness. Other days will be filled with happiness, and joy will abound. Don't beat yourself up because you are having a difficult day and are not feeling happy. Many people in early sobriety assume that any sign of unhappiness is always a relapse symptom. Although chronic unhappiness or negative thinking is absolutely a relapse sign, it is very normal to have short periods of being less than happy. You are human, and human beings experience the entire gamut of emotion in sobriety. Let us face it, happiness is a desired feeling and state of being. We all strive for happiness, but we must not be in denial when we are having an off day or we are in an unhappy mood. I have worked with patients in the past who had a preconceived notion that they could never be unhappy or angry again. They thought that they could not experience any negative emotion again in sobriety. Others believed that all negative feelings were gone for good! I educate my clients concerning the importance of feeling emotions and letting feelings flow freely. It is not dangerous to feel unhappy or angry at times. The way in which a person deals with being in a negative mood can affect him for a lifetime. If he chooses to operate from an unhappy state permanently, he will become extremely negative and will most likely spend time around negative people, places, and things. If he chooses to ignore unhappy thoughts and circumstances, he will live a life of denial and miss opportunity for growth and development. On the other hand, if he chooses to allow feelings of unhappiness to flow, he will provide himself an opportunity to better understand who he is through the experience and will provide a way in which to be more in tune with emotions. I am not saying that it is good to live in negativity and okay to be an unhappy person. I believe that being chronically unhappy is dangerous and a debilitating threat to sobriety. I am simply providing you with a message that it is okay to have moments where you are feeling unhappy. Without these moments, it would be tough to make positive change and to grow as a sober individual. When you are unhappy, it is time to assess the situation and to make things better.

Tina is a twenty-eight year old mother of two. She has been married for three years and is newly in recovery from an addiction to both marijuana and alcohol. She is working her program and attends twelve step support meetings at least three days a week. She has a sponsor. She has a sober support phone list and calls the sober individuals on the list when she feels a craving, or needs to talk to someone who understands where she has been. Her sober support phone list is comprised of more than twenty names and numbers of other addicts and alcoholics from her twelve step support meetings. She has started exercising with her husband and children. They all love the fact that mom is participating in a game of basketball in the evenings. She is getting adequate amounts of sleep at night. Her children are older now and do not keep her up at night. She is trying to improve her diet. She understands that diet is an important part of recovery. She has limited her caffeine and sugar intake, as she now understands that both ingredients may cause her to crave her drugs of choice. She was surprised when she learned that sugar and caffeine where both stimulants that could alter brain chemistry, producing craving. She is willing to do anything that would limit craving, and diet is only part of her plan. She is incorporating relaxation techniques into her schedule during the weekdays and is reading any recovery literature that she finds available. She prays daily and says the Serenity Prayer at least three times a day. She has even started a new hobby with her daughter. They take a scrapbook class every Saturday morning. This provides a healthy outlet for negative energy. She feels good making memories and designing the pages. The only thing Tina struggles with is the fact that she will not allow herself to be unhappy, not even for a minute. She says that she will never experience an angry feeling again. She says she feels great every minute of every day. I truly believe Tina is setting herself up for failure. Although she is working a strong recovery, she is in denial about many feelings. She has buried negative emotion and will not allow herself to experience many of her own feelings. This is not a realistic approach to sobriety, and I am concerned that she will not know how to handle the emotions when they finally boil to the surface. It is impossible to keep the negative feelings bottled forever. They will finally push their way to the surface, and then Tina will have to deal with a much larger problem. When people like Tina do not allow all feelings to flow freely, they run the risk of developing depression, anxiety problems, and most importantly, a relapse with drugs or alcohol. You must acknowledge all feelings and learn to be comfortable in your own skin. If you are having too many unhappy days, you must become aware of this pattern. You must try to understand why you are unhappy and attempt to improve the situation. Is there a specific circumstance causing you to feel unsatisfied? Are you developing a pattern of negative thinking? Negative thinking begets negative feeling and emotions. If you think ugly thoughts constantly, you will feel horrible! When you catch yourself dwelling on negative thoughts and not making any progress in dealing with the thoughts, it is time to focus energy on positive aspects in life. Although you must acknowledge and address negative thoughts as they arise, it is lethal to dwell on negative thoughts! You must send each negative thought through what I refer to as a SOBER EMOTION SCREEN.

SOBER EMOTION SCREEN

1. First, you will acknowledge that you are having a negative thought. If you choose to ignore the thought, it may resurface again at some point and may damage your overall emotional health. Address the issue as it occurs, and then let it dissolve.

2. Next, you must determine whether or not your thought is accurate. Is this thought simply your own assumption, or is it real? If you are hurt because your sister did not compliment your new haircut, you may assume it looks horrible! You may begin to feel unattractive. You must step back, gather your thoughts, and remember that even if she does not like your new hair, it is only her opinion. It is important to be happy with your own opinions, and not to rely on others for feelings of positive self worth. It is possible that she likes your hair, and chose not to mention it. Sometimes you will experience fleeting thoughts that are no real cause for concern. You may lose your keys and tell yourself how stupid you are. You just need to replace these thoughts with positive ones. Practice positive self-talk and remind yourself that you are not stupid, and that everyone misplaces things sometimes. Devise a plan and search for the keys.

3. Choose how you will address the negative thought. Is it best to gently confront the person or situation about which you are having negative thoughts? If someone is hurting you and you are having negative thoughts, perhaps you need to address the issue with this person. Remember to use" I Statements" which relay how you feel concerning the person's behavior. An example of an" I Statement" is as follows: "I feel hurt that you sometimes talk to me in a rough tone." Never blame the person because they will not hear your concern and will feel attacked. For example, you would not want to say "You always talk to me with such a mean voice!" Always begin your concern with how you feel as a result of the inappropriate action or behavior. For effective change the other person needs to understand how you are feeling, and it is important that communication is not perceived as aggressive action.

4. Take some positive action in order to cope with your negative thought. Some positive action steps for coping with the thought and emotion may include the following: journaling thoughts in a diary, discussing thoughts with your sponsor or a sober support, exercising as an outlet for negative energy, drawing or painting each emotion as it occurs, and choosing to think a positive thought for every negative thought that you have. It is good to count your blessings and to think about positive things after dealing with a negative happening or thought. Sometimes, it becomes important to keep track of your emotions. It would be beneficial for you to record your emotions over the next two weeks. Simply begin by drawing in the face that you are feeling today and each day following, as an attempt to track your emotions. For example, if you are happy you will want to create a happy face. Add a smile and even some dots for a pair of eyes. Be creative, and turn each circle into a picture of yourself. Write the date above the face, and give a description as to why you may

be feeling a certain way. Keeping track of emotions is a great way to determine if you are slipping into a pattern of negativity.

HOW AM I FEELING TODAY? USE YOUR CREATIVITY AND DRAW YOUR EMOTION.TURN EACH CIRCLE INTO A FACE OF EXPRESSION AND FEELING! IF YOU ARE FEELING BLUE TODAY,DRAW A SAD FACE IN THE CIRCLE.HOWEVER,IF YOU ARE HAPPY,SIMPLY DRAW A HAPPY FACE IN THE CIRCLE.BE CREATIVE!

Description of feeling_____
Today's date_____

Description of feeling_____
Today's date_____

Description of feeling_____
Today's date_____

Description of feeling_____
Today's date_____

Description of feeling_____
Today's date_____

Description of feeling_____
Today's date_____

Description of feeling_____
Today's date_____

Description of feeling_____
Today's date_____

Description of feeling_____
Today's date_____

Description of feeling_____
Today's date_____

Description of feeling_____
Today's date_____

Description of feeling_____
Today's date_____

Description of feeling_____
Today's date_____

Description of feeling_____
Today's date_____

Description of feeling_____
Today's date_____

After keeping track of your emotions for two weeks, reflect on each face of emotion above and determine if there may be a specific pattern. Are you truly happy all of the time? Or could you be denying some aspect of your emotional health? It is important to be completely honest concerning your feelings and emotions.

Are you really that unhappy everyday? If so, it may be time to consult a professional for assistance. It is important to take positive action if a pattern of negative thinking, feeling, and behaving begins.

If you see a pattern of unhappiness, describe any situations in your life that may be contributing to the emotions._____
_____
_____
_____

_____

_____

Perhaps you illustrated happy faces each day. This can be great! Maybe things are going well, and you are finding happiness each day. Congratulations, if this is the case!

Write about your happiness. List any positive things that have happened to you.

_____

_____

_____

_____

_____

_____

_____

_____

_____

_____

Did you draw happy faces each day, yet are refusing to address painful happenings and emotions? If so, now is time to write about these circumstances. _____

_____

_____

_____

_____

_____

_____

Maybe you had a mixed bag of emotions, which can be very normal. Perhaps you were happy many days and unhappy a few other days. As long as you are working through negative feelings and able to move past them by resolving each feeling, all is probably going well and within the normal range. Write about your mixed bag of emotions._____

_____

_____

_____

_____

_____

_____

_____

_____

List any positive actions that should be made for making affective changes in your mood._____

_____

_____

_____

_____

_____

_____

_____

If you are uncertain concerning ways to make positive changes regarding your mood, it is important to seek professional counsel. Remember that you altered your mood with chemicals, which directly altered your brain chemistry. It is possible to temporarily damage pleasure receptor sites in your brain, and these receptor sites may take time to regenerate. I am suggesting that if you cannot experience happiness at all, it is urgent that you consult a doctor or a therapist! Medication and/or counseling may be recommended. Again, you may want to list at least three counseling agencies or private counselors in your area in the space below. If you already selected a counseling agency, as suggested earlier in this book, it will be best to use the same agency. Remember to find phone numbers in your local phonebook or online. Maybe you know what positive changes need to be made, but are uncertain about how to get started with the process of positive change. Counseling offers an excellent opportunity to move forward in your life. Counselors will help facilitate any unresolved issues and will provide information that is necessary in order to grow emotionally.

1._____

_____

2._____

_____

3._____

_____

Do not forget to call and schedule an appointment as soon as possible!

Some people complain that they are NEVER happy and always bored. This can be a dangerous relapse sign. It is important to create your own happiness. It is necessary to seek happiness from enjoying the simple things in life. Happiness does not just come to you like a birthday package you would receive in the mail. You must work to create your own happiness. Other people can't make you happy. Events can't make you happy. Happiness is within yourself. You must stay in touch with feelings in order to resolve difficulty as it arises. Feelings are a blessing. Think about periods in your life where you have felt excited or filled with extreme joy. You must allow yourself to feel the emotions. If you numb yourself with alcohol or drugs, you miss these experiences. If you self medicate with chemicals, you do not grow on an emotional level and are not able to work through identity issues and life struggles. It is important to remember that working through the tough times makes a person stronger and builds character.

Write about a time during which you allowed yourself to feel great joy and excitement._____

_____
_____
_____
_____
_____
_____
_____
_____
_____
_____
_____

Write about a time during which you allowed yourself to feel sorrow and pain.

_____
_____
_____
_____
_____
_____
_____
_____
_____
_____

How did you grow from these experiences?_____

_____
_____
_____
_____

How will you start enjoying the simple pleasures of life? I have compiled a list of simple pleasures. Please read through the list and place a check next to the pleasures that appeal to you. Feel free to add to the list.

1. Drink tea on the patio as you watch the beautiful sunrise.
2. Chase butterflies with your child.
3. Smell a flower and concentrate on the aroma.
4. Play in the rain.
5. When you notice a rainbow, focus on the color of the rainbow that reflects your personality.
6. Build a sandcastle.
7. Pet your dog for more than 5 minutes.
8. Sing silly songs with your children.
9. Hang a hammock in your yard and actually lie in it at the end of the day.
10. Plant a tree.
11. Close your eyes while listening to your favorite tune.
12. Enjoy a bubble bath.
13. Smell the rain before and after a storm.
14. Create your favorite dish and savor every bite.
15. Enjoy a lollipop.
16. Watch children play.
17. Enjoy a bicycle ride on a breezy day.
18. Make pictures out of clouds in the sky.
19. Run your fingers through a baby's fine hair.
20. Hug a friend and enjoy the moment.
21. Smile at someone special.
22. Build a snowman.
23. Blow bubbles.
24. Roast marshmallows.
25. Fly a kite.
26. Read poetry.
27. Write in a journal.
28. Paint a picture.
29. Color with your children.
30. Picnic in the park.
31. Take a drive in the country.
32. Collect seashells on the beach.
33. Gather fresh flowers for your home.

34. Eat dinner by candlelight.
35. Gaze upon the moon and stars.
36. Dance to your favorite music.
37. Spend time looking at old photos.
38. Fish in your favorite body of water.
39. Take pictures of the sunset.
40. Paint your bedroom your favorite color.
41. Call an old friend.
42. Enjoy the scent of freshly cut grass.
43. Sit on a porch swing.
44. Catch lightening bugs.
45. Heat bath towels and pajamas on a cold night.
46. Savor a warm cup of hot chocolate.
47. Make and enjoy homemade ice cream.
48. Watch your favorite comedy and laugh out loud.
49. Skip pebbles across the surface of a lake.
50. Build a fire and feel the warmth.

List any additional simple pleasures that you might enjoy.

51.
52.
53.
54.
55.

When you understand the importance of creating your happiness, living a sober lifestyle really becomes fun. Sometimes in the hustle and rush of life you forget to enjoy simple pleasures, and you tend to focus on the stressors in your life. Although you do have to address stressors, you do not have to stay there. You have the power in your sober life to choose your own attitude. You can create happiness within yourself. When you were using chemicals, the only thing that mattered to you were drugs and alcohol. They only provided a false sense of security. You needed an escape from feelings and emotions. Today, you want to understand who you are, and you desire to grow emotionally. You are sober and free to make our own decisions. Today, you must decide to learn to live again. Creating your own happiness makes the journey a little sweeter.

It is important to have "AN ATTITUDE OF GRATITUDE" each day. I think it is important to begin each day with a prayer and to focus on gratitude. Choose AN "ATTITUDE OF GRATITUDE" again at night before you go to sleep. I started the "ATTITUDE OF GRATITUDE" with each of my children when negative thinking and behaving became too much in my home. My kids were starting to complain and bicker about small things, and I knew how damaging little negative complaints could be to a person's well being. I wanted my children to focus on the positives in their lives before bedtime each night. My three children and I continue to practice the "ATTITUDE OF GRATITUDE" still today. After bedtime prayers, we all huddle together and chant "ATTITUDE OF GRATITUDE". My children look forward to our little huddle and our "ATTITUDE OF GRATITUDE" each evening. If I forget, my eight year old daughter will remind us to give thanks. I have noticed that my children are more positive now, and do not dwell on the negatives in life. I want to encourage you to choose an "ATTITUDE OF GRATITUDE" for your life. If you have children or grandchildren, you may want to try this positive thinking exercise with them. Or you may wish to begin an "ATTITUDE OF GRATITUDE" journal in which you record your blessings. You may even just silently remember your "ATTITUDE OF GRATITUDE" each day. It is best to choose a specific time during which you will reflect on your blessings, so that it becomes a healthy habit.

Will you choose an "ATTITUDE OF GRATITUDE" for your life? What are you thankful for today?

CHAPTER 4

HOW DO I DEAL WITH
GUILT AND SHAME?

Megan was only two years old when she was reprimanded for accidentally spilling her chocolate milk. Her mother told her she was bad and should not have spilled her milk.

John was just fourteen years old when he was grounded for making too many mistakes on his math test. His dad told him that he was stupid and needed to earn better scores on exams.

Mary was eight years old when she was shamed for forgetting her coat at school. Her mother pointed out that her sister would never do something so irresponsible! Bruce was ten years old when his father yelled at him for leaving his bike outside in the driveway. His father called him an idiot and made him cry with his loud and harsh tone of voice.

All of the examples listed above are situations in which parents shame their children. All of the children were hurt by the comments. Human beings are incapable of being perfect and will always make mistakes. When a child is wrong, he should be corrected in a healthy manner. For example, Bruce's father could have given him a consequence for leaving his bike outside. Removing a privilege would have served as a healthy punishment for leaving his bike outside. No child should be scolded for accidentally spilling milk. Megan, at just two years of age received the message that she was a bad girl! This message is not healthy for Megan's self esteem, and if the messages continue, they will severely affect her feelings of self worth later in life.

Describe any shame messages that you received as a child._____
_____
_____
_____
_____
_____
_____
_____
_____

_____
_____
_____
_____
_____
_____
_____

Can you recall how the messages made you feel during that time period? Do those messages still bother you today? Describe._____
_____
_____
_____
_____
_____
_____
_____
_____
_____
_____

Guilt is a healthy and normal response to any action that we know is not right. If a person steals money from his grandmother for drugs, it is a healthy response for him to feel guilty after committing the crime. Feelings of guilt and shame are normal and help prevent people from repeating the undesirable behavior. However, when drugs and alcohol become the first love in a person's life, guilt does not always prevent him from doing wrong. When the person continues to repeat the wrong behavior, the guilt and shame grow deeper.

Write about a time during which you felt guilty for your action, yet kept repeating the wrong behavior._____

_____
_____
_____
_____
_____
_____
_____
_____
_____
_____
_____
_____

_____

_____

_____

_____

_____

_____

There are two types of shame. HEALTHY SHAME is actually important in healthy sober development because it is an emotion that allows one to be human. Shame helps us understand that we are not God. Shame helps us learn about limits. We must understand that we cannot do everything perfectly. Sometimes we need to ask for help. Without healthy shame we would not have values and morals. We would not feel guilty about wrong behaviors. TOXIC SHAME is dangerous! When one feels guilty and shamed most all of the time, it can become a state of being. Shame can become the person's entire identity. This person feels flawed as a human being. He believes he is a failure and can do nothing right. This person sees himself as unworthy of love and respect and may even view himself as being fundamentally bad. Toxic shame blocks healthy human development.

Many people feel toxic shame in their lives, yet struggle with the reasons why they are filled with such pain and dysfunction. Toxic shame is developed through significant relationships. Sources of toxic shame may include: criticism and harsh discipline from parents, sibling jealousy and comparisons, spousal abuse, and peer pressure. In all of these relationships a person is made to feel worthless and inadequate. When a child is shamed throughout childhood, he is likely to feel that he must deserve the abuse. He may believe the abuse he experiences is all his fault. As an adult, the same child will most likely continue to feel inadequate as a person. He will wonder who will love him, and who he can trust. He will have many abandonment issues. He will wonder who he can depend on in life. He will probably get into relationships with other shame—based people and pass on shameless behavior to his own children. Dysfunctional cycles tend to repeat with every generation. The repetition continues until someone breaks the cycle by learning positive ways in which to cope with pain and conflict.

Write about any toxic shame present in your life._____

_____

_____

_____

_____

_____

_____

_____

_____
_____
_____
_____

Shame is recognized in several ways. The most obvious indicators of shame include physical signs, such as, lowered eyes, poor eye contact, down-cast head, and flushing neck and face. Mental symptoms include: self-criticism, poor self image, a negative attitude, and devaluing of self. Spiritual symptoms include disconnection from self, inability to connect with others, and loss of connection with a higher power. Behavioral symptoms consist of the following: addiction, perfectionism, and criticism. Shame-based individuals learn to rely on things outside of themselves for a temporary escape. Addictions of chemical dependency, gambling, shopping, sex, food, and work typically provide the very temporary escape. People with addictions seek to numb painful feelings and want to forget about shameful messages. These cover-ups/dependencies often lead to deeper shame.

Describe how you covered up toxic shame with your own addiction._____
_____
_____
_____
_____

COMMON SHAME MESSAGES

SHAME ON YOU!
YOU ARE SO STUPID.
YOU WILL NEVER AMOUNT TO ANYTHING.
IT IS ALL YOUR FAULT!
WHY CAN'T YOU BE MORE LIKE YOUR BROTHER?
YOU ARE NOT GOOD ENOUGH.
HOW COULD YOU DO THIS?
YOU OWE IT TO ME!
I WILL NOT LOVE YOU IF . . .
YOU DO NOT REALLY FEEL LIKE THAT . . . .
THAT DIDN'T HURT, SO DON"T CRY.
I CAN'T BELIEVE YOU DID THAT!
YOU ARE JUST LIKE YOUR FATHER!

Have you ever received any of the above shameful messages? Describe feelings associated with the messages._____
_____
_____

_____
_____
_____
_____
_____
_____
_____

Many shame-based people believe that they are doomed for life. They think they will always be filled with shame and guilt. They feel trapped and often relapse because they simply cannot deal with the painful emotions. In reality, relapse only adds to the shame and makes a person's life more painful. A shame-based person must strive to overcome the toxic shame and learn healthy ways in which to cope with the dysfunction.

There are several steps necessary in order to heal from toxic shame.

1. A person must surrender or give up control. Many people choose to surrender to a higher power. They recognize that they are only human and that they need God to guide and direct their lives. Prayer can be an effective way in which to surrender and to heal the hole in a person's soul.

2. A person needs a connection with others. It is important not to hide from the pain in isolation from people. Build relationships with people who are positive influences. It is important to have sober supports who can listen to your concerns. Sponsor support and group or individual therapy are extremely helpful.

3. Expressing old pain is necessary in order for a person to understand why he may react in certain ways today. It hurts to look at painful pasts, but it is the key to unlocking a healthy future. I would strongly recommend that a person seek professional help for an abusive past. It is therapeutic to process emotions with a trained professional.

4. Self-love is important. Remember that love is not a feeling, but a commitment. You must make a decision to treat yourself with the respect that you deserve! Following through with this commitment will not be an easy task and will take practice. Just keep reminding yourself daily that you are worth it!

5. Positive Self-Talk is vital for healthy human development. You must learn to replace old shameful messages with positive affirmations.

The following are healthy affirmations that you may incorporate into your own life:

- I AM ALLOWED TO BE ANGRY.
- IT IS OKAY FOR ME TO TAKE RISKS AND INVEST IN NEW RELATIONSHIPS.
- I AM BEAUTIFUL JUST THE WAY I AM!

- I AM ALLOWED TO MAKE MISTAKES.
- I CAN SET HEALTHY BOUNDARIES WITH OTHERS.
- I CAN PROTECT MYSELF PHYSICALLY, EMOTIONALLY, AND SPIRITUALLY.
- I CAN ENJOY MY LIFE.
- I CAN TAKE CARE OF MYSELF.
- I AM ALLOWED TO CRY WHEN I HURT.
- I AM A POSITIVE PERSON.
- I AM WORTHY AND LOVABLE.
- I CAN EXPRESS MY OWN FEELINGS.
- I AM SMART.
- I MAKE GOOD DECISIONS.
- IT IS OKAY TO NOT FEEL GUILTY.
- I AM STRONG AND COMFORTABLE IN MY OWN SKIN.
- I CAN CHANGE MY OWN MIND.
- I CAN TRUST MY OWN JUDGEMENT.

It feels good to talk to yourself in a positive way. It may seem silly at first, but I encourage you to practice positive affirmations in a mirror. Stand in front of a mirror each morning and tell yourself why you are important. Eventually you will just automatically think the positive affirmations and may not need to say them out loud.

Express ways in which you are important. Identify your own positive affirmations.

_____
_____
_____
_____
_____
_____
_____
_____
_____
_____
_____
_____
_____
_____
_____
_____

Do not forget to practice your affirmations each morning and then several times throughout the day. It is okay to feel awkward doing this at first. Just remind yourself of your commitment to love yourself.

CHAPTER 5

IS IT OKAY TO BE ANGRY?

Many people in early recovery, struggle with angry feelings. Some individuals assume that it is not okay to be angry in sobriety. Several people feel so guilty that they return to using chemicals again in order to numb the feelings. Others fight the angry thoughts for a while and experience a level of denial. These people deny that they feel any angry feelings and will use distractions to avoid situations or people that may become associated with angry feelings. I have personally worked with alcoholics and addicts who would force a smile and tell me that everything was wonderful, when I could see from their nonverbal behavior that this was simply not the case. Although people can hide or deny angry feelings for a while, it will not work forever. Picture a smoldering volcano for a moment or two. Do you have a clear picture in your mind? What do you see? I see hot lava and ash, and I watch closely for an eruption. It is easy to compare angry feelings that are denied expression to a volcano that could erupt any day. You see, for a short time period you may really believe that all is well and always will be. This is sometimes referred to as a honeymoon phase. If you are married or have ever been in love, you will understand this term. The first few months of a relationship are usually marvelous. You only focus on the good in your mate and you feel a "high" or a feeling of infatuation. Eventually reality sets in, and you may notice that your mate is not perfect. You realize that you still have to pay bills, and the honeymoon eventually dissolves. This does not mean that the love fizzles and there is no chance for true love. True love is a commitment and is not always a feeling. In true love you recognize that you will not always feel ecstatic. There will be times that you will be angry with your mate. This is true about life in general. It is as normal to feel angry emotions as it is to experience feelings of happiness. If you go into a relationship with a goal of never arguing or having any disagreements, you are clearly setting yourself up for failure. If you deny angry feelings, you will eventually boil over, just like the volcano you may still have pictured in your mind. It is of prime importance to manage anger effectively in recovery. Managing anger will help to keep you on the path of sobriety and will make your life more peaceful and fulfilling.

Describe a time when you tried to deny angry feelings._____

_____

Have you ever erupted like a volcano with angry thoughts and feelings?_____

_____

You may be wondering exactly what anger is. Many people believe anger is bad and wrong. They think anger is a full-blown rage. Many believe anger to be dangerous. If anger was considered to be a full-blown rage, we would all be in trouble. It is easy to see why many people try to deny angry feelings, as they have such negative views about anger. The following three words sum up the meaning of anger: HURT, FEAR, AND REJECTION.

Anger is not rage! Feeling angry and acting angry are two entirely different things. It would not be appropriate or healthy to fly into a temper tantrum because you feel mad. Perhaps you have done this. Think about a toddler that you know. Have you ever seen the child throw a temper tantrum? All three of my children have thrown a temper tantrum or two. Children have to learn how to manage anger, just like my own children had to learn at an early age.

Describe a time when you threw a temper tantrum or flew into a mad rage._____

_____

_____

_____

_____

_____

_____

_____

_____

_____

_____

Did you believe that the angry outburst was effective? What happened following
the outburst? Describe feelings associated with the experience._____

_____

_____

_____

_____

_____

_____

_____

_____

_____

_____

_____

_____

Did you hurt anyone during or following the anger outburst? Describe._____

_____

_____

_____

_____

When you begin to feel angry learn to ask yourself the following question: Do I feel
hurt, scared, or rejected?

Describe something or someone who currently triggers you to experience angry
emotions._____

_____

_____

_____

_____

_____
_____
_____
_____
_____
_____
_____
_____

Ponder on your answer for a moment and explore any areas of hurt, fear, and rejection. Describe. _____

_____
_____
_____
_____
_____
_____
_____
_____
_____
_____
_____
_____

Perhaps you are wondering if you can just choose not to be angry and somehow learn to avoid the hassle of learning to manage conflict. The answer is NO! If a person chooses to suppress anger in an attempt to avoid the emotion, he will often feel depressed. Anger turned inward will lead to feelings of hopelessness and depressed mood. Holding anger in can lead to both mental and physical illness.

Gail is a twenty-six year old mother of two young children. She has been in recovery from alcohol dependency for three years. She is married, although her husband works most of the time and is seldom home to help her with household chores and childcare. When he is not at work, he spends a lot of time playing golf with friends. Gail has a part time job at a local fitness center, which allows her to bring her children to work with her every day. The fitness center has a childcare facility on site, and a benefit of her job is free childcare while she works to earn extra income for the family. Most days it is especially difficult for her to get both kids dressed and out the door on time. Recently, she has been late to work and may be penalized if tardiness continues. She feels stressed due to having too many responsibilities and demands as a mother. She has to cook, clean, take care of her children, mow the lawn, and work four days a week. She continues to make time for two twelve step meetings per week amidst the chaos of her family life. She knows that without the support of other addicts and alcoholics she runs the risk of relapsing. She is extremely irritable with her children and resents her husband's lack of concern and consideration for the family. She feels that he should be around more in order to help with the children and household responsibilities. Although she is angry, she has always stuffed her angry emotions and does not confront her husband concerning the matter. She cries often and feels sad when he is not around to witness her true feelings. She experiences headaches frequently, which are most likely a result of burying angry feelings. If Gail continues to hide from her emotions without making any positive changes, she will become both physically and emotionally ill, and, most importantly, is unknowingly setting herself up for a relapse.

If a person simply chooses not to give much thought to angry feelings, he runs the risk of the following: physically abusing others, making impulsive outbursts, relapsing on chemicals, and taking angry feelings out on safer targets. For example, yelling at his spouse or children when he is really angry with his employer.

Before you can learn to manage angry feelings, you must first learn to recognize when you are angry. There are numerous signs and symptoms of anger.

PHYSICAL SYMPTOMS OF ANGER:

- face feels hot or flushed
- clench jaw or grind teeth
- blood pressure increases
- heart beats faster
- headaches
- clench fists
- tap feet
- voice becomes louder
- dry throat and throat may feel tight
- stomachaches
- feeling of an "adrenaline rush"
- difficulty sleeping
- stiff neck and tense muscles
- nail biting
- shallow breathing
- violent outbursts

EMOTIONAL SYMPTOMS OF ANGER:

- frequent crying episodes
- feelings of depressed mood
- irritability
- low frustration tolerance
- mood swings

- anxiety
- feeling rejected
- sarcasm
- being overly critical of self and others
- apathy
- blaming others
- recurrent self-pity
- lethargy

SPIRITUAL SYMPTOMS OF ANGER:

- lack of self-esteem
- fear of others
- not having a purpose for being
- unhappy with higher power
- lack of compassion and understanding
- lack of respect for others
- lack of courage and strength
- lack of spiritual activities, such as praying or meditation
- lack of honesty and integrity
- isolation from others

Describe your own physical symptoms of anger._____

_____

_____

_____

_____

_____

_____

_____

_____

_____

Describe any emotional symptoms of anger that you have experienced recently.

_____

_____

_____

_____

_____

_____

_____

_____

_____

_____

Have you experienced any spiritual symptoms of being angry?_____

_____

_____

_____

_____

_____

_____

_____

_____

_____

Although feeling angry from time to time is healthy and normal, it is a negative energy in your mind and body that must be released in healthy ways in order to mature in recovery. One who chooses to act violently will only exacerbate feelings of anger and may put self and others in danger. It is extremely important to manage anger effectively. There are several important strategies that are helpful when learning to effectively cope with angry feelings. You must choose the best strategies for yourself.

*Exercise is probably one of the most therapeutic ways to release anger energy. Exercise may increase serotonin and dopamine in the brain, which are essential brain chemicals necessary for a sober lifestyle. Some exercise activities to consider may include: tennis, bicycling, walking, running, karate, basketball, swimming, and aerobics. I am sure that you could add to the list with other healthy exercise choices.

Is exercise an important part of your life? Describe current exercise habits._____

_____

_____

_____

_____

_____

_____

Please indicate at least one exercise activity in which you would like to become involved._____

_____

_____

_____

_____

_____

_____

It is important to check with your family doctor before beginning any exercise program. Vigorous exercise may be dangerous if you are not in good health. Schedule a check up today if you have not done so already. When was your last medical exam? Have you been okayed by a doctor to start any new exercise?_____

_____

_____

_____

*Journaling is a wonderful way in which to release anger energy. Writing is a healthy form of expression. It is a great idea to journal on a daily basis. You may express feelings of happiness as well as angry emotions in your journal.

*Art is another valuable way to cope with angry feelings. Pencil drawings, paint, chalk, and clay are appropriate mediums in which to express yourself. Sometimes it is safer to paint or to sculpt our feelings in a nonverbal manner, rather than express ourselves verbally.

*Music is a relaxing way to calm angry feelings. Sometimes singing along with the radio in a loud voice can be a healthy form of anger expression. Singing relieves tension and provides a healthy outlet for the release of energy.

*Talk Therapy is a valuable way in which to cope with negative energy. It may be important to consult with an individual psychotherapist in order to facilitate complicated anger. It is extremely necessary to have regular contact with a sponsor who shares your desire for recovery.

Do you have a sponsor? Do you talk to your sponsor about angry feelings? Describe.

_____

_____

_____

_____

Twelve step meeting attendance is an opportunity to talk to others who genuinely share your goals for long-term sobriety.

Do you attend twelve step meetings regularly? How often do you attend meetings?

_____

_____

_____

Do you have a best friend in whom you can confide? Write about your relationship.

_____

_____

_____

_____

_____

_____

_____

*Forgiveness is a huge way to lift feelings of anger! It is much more difficult and damaging to hold on to resentments and wrongdoings. You must remember that forgiving does not mean that you must forget and deny the person's responsibility in his wrong actions. It means that you will not hold the other person in debt of the wrongdoing. Being open and honest with the person whom you decide to forgive is an important part of forgiving. Encourage the person to take responsibility for his actions and then make the decision to let bitter feelings dissolve. You will feel relieved and uplifted!

Is there someone you need to forgive? Are you ready to commit to forgiving this person?_____

_____

_____

_____

_____

Remember that you have to choose to forgive on your own timetable when you are truly ready to forgive! Keep in mind that the longer you allow anger to fester, the more likely the bitterness may harm you. Make a solid effort to understand your own anger. It is important to pay attention to any angry feelings on a daily basis. Record angry thoughts for approximately two weeks in the ANGER LOG. Record the ways in which you respond to anger in each situation.

ANGER LOG

TODAY'S DATE:

I AM ANGRY BECAUSE:

PHYSICAL SYMPTOMS OF MY ANGER INCLUDE:

EMOTIONAL SYMPTOMS OF MY ANGER INCLUDE:

SPIRITUAL SYMPTOMS OF MY ANGER INCLUDE:

HOW I COPED WITH MY ANGRY FEELINGS:

TODAY'S DATE:

I AM ANGRY BECAUSE:

PHYSICAL SYMPTOMS OF MY ANGER INCLUDE:

EMOTIONAL SYMPTOMS OF MY ANGER INCLUDE:

SPIRITUAL SYMPTOMS OF MY ANGER INCLUDE:

HOW I COPED WITH MY ANGRY FEELINGS:

TODAY'S DATE:

I AM ANGRY BECAUSE:

PHYSICAL SYMPTOMS OF MY ANGER INCLUDE:

EMOTIONAL SYMPTOMS OF MY ANGER INCLUDE:

SPIRITUAL SYMPTOMS OF MY ANGER INCLUDE:

HOW I COPED WITH MY ANGRY FEELINGS:

TODAY'S DATE:

I AM ANGRY BECAUSE:

PHYSICAL SYMPTOMS OF MY ANGER INCLUDE:

EMOTIONAL SYMPTOMS OF MY ANGER INCLUDE:

SPIRITUAL SYMPTOMS OF MY ANGER INCLUDE:

HOW I COPED WITH MY ANGRY FEELINGS:

TODAY'S DATE:

I AM ANGRY BECAUSE:

PHYSICAL SYMPTOMS OF MY ANGER INCLUDE:

EMOTIONAL SYMPTOMS OF MY ANGER INCLUDE:

SPIRITUAL SYMPTOMS OF MY ANGER INCLUDE:

HOW I COPED WITH MY ANGRY FEELINGS:

TODAY'S DATE:

I AM ANGRY BECAUSE:

PHYSICAL SYMPTOMS OF MY ANGER INCLUDE:

EMOTIONAL SYMPTOMS OF MY ANGER INCLUDE:

SPIRITUAL SYMPTOMS OF MY ANGER INCLUDE:

HOW I COPED WITH MY ANGRY FEELINGS:

TODAY'S DATE:

I AM ANGRY BECAUSE:

PHYSICAL SYMPTOMS OF MY ANGER INCLUDE:

EMOTIONAL SYMPTOMS OF MY ANGER INCLUDE:

SPIRITUAL SYMPTOMS OF MY ANGER INCLUDE:

HOW I COPED WITH MY ANGRY FEELINGS:

TODAY'S DATE:

I AM ANGRY BECAUSE:

PHYSICAL SYMPTOMS OF MY ANGER INCLUDE:

EMOTIONAL SYMPTOMS OF MY ANGER INCLUDE:

SPIRITUAL SYMPTOMS OF MY ANGER INCLUDE:

HOW I COPED WITH MY ANGRY FEELINGS:

TODAY'S DATE:

I AM ANGRY BECAUSE:

PHYSICAL SYMPTOMS OF MY ANGER INCLUDE:

EMOTIONAL SYMPTOMS OF MY ANGER INCLUDE:

SPIRITUAL SYMPTOMS OF MY ANGER INCLUDE:

HOW I COPED WITH MY ANGRY FEELINGS:

TODAY'S DATE:

I AM ANGRY BECAUSE:

PHYSICAL SYMPTOMS OF MY ANGER INCLUDE:

EMOTIONAL SYMPTOMS OF MY ANGER INCLUDE:

SPIRITUAL SYMPTOMS OF MY ANGER INCLUDE:

HOW I COPED WITH MY ANGRY FEELINGS:

TODAY'S DATE:

I AM ANGRY BECAUSE:

PHYSICAL SYMPTOMS OF MY ANGER INCLUDE:

EMOTIONAL SYMPTOMS OF MY ANGER INCLUDE:

SPIRITUAL SYMPTOMS OF MY ANGER INCLUDE:

HOW I COPED WITH MY ANGRY FEELINGS:

TODAY'S DATE:

I AM ANGRY BECAUSE:

PHYSICAL SYMPTOMS OF MY ANGER INCLUDE:

EMOTIONAL SYMPTOMS OF MY ANGER INCLUDE:

SPIRITUAL SYMPTOMS OF MY ANGER INCLUDE:

HOW I COPED WITH MY ANGRY FEELINGS:

After taking time to assess any angry moments, evaluate whether or not you chose appropriate ways to cope with angry emotions.

Discuss healthy ways in which you chose to handle your angry feelings._____
_____
_____
_____
_____
_____
_____

_____

Describe unhealthy or destructive ways you chose to express angry emotions._____
_____
_____
_____
_____
_____
_____
_____
_____

_____

If you chose an unhealthy way to express anger, identify a healthy replacement for the destructive expression of anger._____

_____

If you chose healthy alternatives to handle angry feelings, identify ways in which your anger expression helped you to cope with the situation in positive ways.

_____

If you notice a clear pattern of angry thoughts, and you are continuing to deal with anger in unhealthy ways, it would be best for you to consult a local professional for further direction. Inappropriate anger expression can be extremely dangerous to everyone, and is not to be taken lightly. In a small number of cases, anger can be a serious psychological problem that requires professional treatment. In many cases, however, people have learned dysfunctional ways to cope with anger, and simply do not make any efforts to replace the undesirable behaviors with appropriate and healthy strategies. It is your choice to decide to handle angry emotions in healthy ways. It may take practice before healthy replacements feel good. Be patient and understand that you are helping yourself and others by choosing healthy ways for coping with anger. Expressing anger appropriately is an important part of recovery.

CHAPTER 6

HOW DO I DEAL WITH STRESS?

Are you wondering if searching for your sober self is too stressful? It is true that you will have to put much effort into your recovery and your search for identity. I challenge you to view this time as an adventure. Although it can be stressful to explore painful emotions, it can sometimes be equally as stressful to experience happy emotions. You will experience both negative and positive stressors in life, which is a normal part of growth and development in recovery. Stressors do not make you sick and keep you trapped in the cycle of addiction, but an inability to appropriately deal with the stressors causes pain. It is an important part of recovery to know how to tackle stressors in life. Let us distinguish between positive and negative stressors for a moment. Some examples of negative stressors are: losing your job, divorce, death of a loved one, illness, relationship difficulties, and parenting a wayward child. Examples of positive stressors include: marriage, a new job, birth of a baby, relocating to a new area, and purchasing a new home. Positive stress causes you to become excited, which produces a brief physical change in your body. Your heart rate and blood pressure increase slightly, and you experience a short-lived adrenaline rush. The same "fight or flight" response occurs in your body during negative stress. Keep in mind that if you experience this stress response for long periods of time, you are subject to both physical and mental illness. If you experience a prolonged stress—reaction and do not have periods from which to recover, you may become depressed or anxious. You may suffer from decreased immune function, which can cause a greater susceptibility to colds, viruses, and infections. You might relapse and return to drinking and drugging if stressors are not effectively handled in a timely fashion. The good news is that there are numerous ways in which to cope with stressors in life! Remember that stressors do not cause illness, but unhealthy reactions to stressors are the culprit. There are many people with a great deal of stress in their lives who are doing well. There are other people who are subject to very little stress, yet cannot seem to cope.

Identify positive stress that you are currently experiencing._____

_____

_____

_____
_____
_____
_____
_____
_____
_____
_____

Are you enduring negative stress in your life presently?_____
_____
_____
_____
_____
_____
_____
_____
_____
_____
_____

How has your reaction to stress affected your overall health and sobriety?_____
_____
_____
_____
_____
_____
_____
_____
_____

I would like to demonstrate several different strategies that explain how individuals respond to stress in their lives. I will use sports to illustrate my examples. Please do not assume that I am biased and have a favorite sport based on my analogies, as I do not. All five sports examples that I will use are equally important sports in which to participate. As a matter of fact, my youngest daughter plays soccer and loves the sport. My son plays basketball, and we often play this sport together as a family. My husband and brother are avid golfers. My sister-in-law likes nothing more than a good game of baseball. My parents absolutely love the game of football, and even purchase tickets to the University of Kentucky football games. As you can see, all five of these sports are an important part of my life. I simply would like to refer to these sports as an illustration of different ways in which individuals respond to stress. Imagine how you respond to stress in the game of life. Picture the ball as the stressor, and the sport as a common way of dealing with stress.

FOOTBALL: Okay, those who deal with stress as in the game of football respond aggressively and attack problems in a rough and aggressive manner. They tackle problems at the expense of injuring or hurting others. These people will run over others in order to win. They see the answer to fighting stress as an attack strategy. A person who deals with life in this way often adds to his stress reaction by coping with stress inappropriately.

Have you ever experienced so much stress that you took it out on others physically or emotionally?_____

_____

_____

_____

_____

_____

_____

_____

_____

Do you or someone you know often respond to stress in this way?_____

_____

_____

_____

_____

_____

_____

_____

_____

How is this coping style damaging?_____

_____

_____

_____

_____

_____

_____

_____

_____

An alcoholic or addict who responds to stress as in the game of football may be angry about his addiction. The alcoholic or addict may verbally attack family members or friends in an attempt to aggressively block out the pain. He may attack anyone who refers to his illness. This person is typically very angry inside and attacks others in an attempt to feel better. In reality this "attacking others" strategy will only add fuel to rage.

Tom is a thirty-six year old addict who has abstained from chemicals for two months now. He continues to deal inappropriately with the stress of life. He refuses to attend twelve step meetings or to attain sponsor support because he does not want to talk about his feelings. He thinks the meetings are for weak individuals who are not strong enough to be sober on their own. He is hurt that others in his life know that he is an addict. He is scared to feel emotion and he feels frustrated by common stressors of life. Tom is irritable, depressed, and miserable all the time. He fails to recognize that he is not truly in recovery. He assumes that he can be sober on his own without the support of others. He does not understand that attempting recovery alone is very frightening and will always cause failure. Tom is lashing out at his wife and children all of the time. He uses his family for a safe target and inappropriately vents his anger and stress in a dangerous manner. He has even acted aggressively toward his wife a few times. His children have suffered verbal abuse from their father and will most likely suffer long-term effects from the trauma. He refuses to talk about his pain and will not discuss the disease of addiction with anyone! Tom's stress reaction is unhealthy and dangerous. If he continues to cope with stress as in the game of football, any personal growth in recovery will remain nonexistent, and he will experience extreme consequences for his actions.

BASEBALL: A person who copes with life as in the game of baseball will give up easily. He will swing at problems a few times, but if he is out at three, he will sit on the bench.

For example, a person who attempts to deal with a stressor in a healthy manner, may discover that it is a lot of work, and quickly give up as a result. This individual feels it is easier to walk away from problems. Problems will eventually come back and occupy space in the mind, so it is best to deal with matters as they arise. A person dealing with life as in the game of baseball will steal bases for the win. In other words, he may take shortcuts in dealing with life stressors. He will avoid situations that may cause him to feel uncomfortable or emotional. This "avoidance strategy" is not a productive way to press forward in the search for identity.

Gavin is a twenty-five year old recovering addict who tends to give up rather than choosing to work through problems. He is currently enrolled in an Intensive Outpatient Treatment Facility where he attends group at least three days a week for three hours each session. He is very good about making it to every outpatient meeting, yet refuses to attend required twelve step meetings. Due to his fear of uncovering a painful past, he is very reluctant to look inward at self. Gavin believes that the twelve step meetings cause him to feel vulnerable. His therapist has tried to give Gavin ample opportunity to open up in group and to explore feelings that are common in everyday life. He would rather look away and smile as if nothing is ever wrong. He buries issues that trigger emotion and works hard to remain neutral. Do you see how denying his feelings could negatively impact his recovery? It is important that Gavin begin to explore his emotions as he must reconnect with his sober identity.

Have you ever responded to stressors in life as in the game of baseball? What were you attempting to avoid? _____

_____

_____

_____

_____

_____

_____

_____

_____

_____

_____

GOLF: A good golfer knows that concentration is necessary before swinging the club. Golf is a relaxed game of concentration and precision. A person who deals with life as in a game of golf, concentrates on the stressor before swinging or deciding how to effectively cope with the issue. This person handles stressors with a relaxed state of mind, taking time to focus on each concern. The golfer is usually even keel and likes to plan appropriate strategies for coping with stress. This person avoids reacting to stress in a swift manner, and takes his time in order to maintain a strong and positive attitude. A person who responds to stress in this way has the knowledge to decrease his reaction to the stressor, and he refuses to allow stress to overpower him.

Faith is a forty-one year old recovering alcoholic. She is married and is a mother of three small children. She works full time and attends twelve step support meetings regularly in order to solidify her recovery. She is very busy, yet manages her time effectively. She carefully plans meals, childcare, and the budgeting of family finances.

Faith's husband usually helps with household chores and assists with childcare. Life is not easy for Faith, yet she chooses to view her sober life as positive and tackles each problem as it arises, but only after careful assessment and planning. She and her husband work as a team, although Faith tends to be the spouse who orchestrates healthy coping strategies for family stressors. Faith understands the importance of planning coping strategies for each individual stressor without overreacting. Faith feels secure in her own person and continues to grow emotionally, as she does not allow life stressors to weigh her down. She chooses to deal appropriately with every issue and always maintains a positive attitude, despite the severity of the stress. She leans on God for strength in times of stress.

Do you deal with stress as in the game of golf? How does this coping style foster emotional and spiritual growth and development in sobriety?_____

SOCCER: A person who deals with stress as in a game of soccer is somewhat fearful of facing obstacles. This person attempts to kick around the stressor, yet never gets his hand on the ball, or the real concern. He kicks around the issue, but is too fearful to truly confront the problem.

Aaron is a thirty-eight year old recovering alcoholic who exhibits much fear in dealing with conflict. Although he is in recovery, he continues to deny other aspects of his mental health. He takes care of himself physically, but absolutely denies that he has any problems. He kicks around problems for a few moments and then decides they are too scary to deal with, so he will deny that the problem exists. Aaron must recognize how important it is to deal with conflict as it presents itself. Currently, he shrugs his shoulders and denies that anything is ever wrong. He does not want to "feel", so he ignores concerns in an attempt to trick reality. In active addiction, Aaron would numb problems with alcohol. In recovery, he has been eating sugar and carbohydrates which seem to dull his pain. He has no idea that negative stressors must be dealt with head on in order to stay sober and to truly discover his sober self. Emotional eating is dangerous, as it will hinder growth and threaten Aaron's newfound sobriety. In order to become healthy, Aaron must not deny that negative stressors exist. He must acknowledge pain and must cope in appropriate ways.

Have you ever dealt with issues as in the game of soccer?_____
_____
_____
_____
_____

BASKETBALL: Now let's explore how a person deals with life stressors as in a game of basketball. A person who copes with life as in the game of basketball hurries down the court, or the game of life, and is careful not to foul or hurt anyone. He simply concentrates on the basket and a win. This person never gives up when his opponent tries to steal the ball for the win. He believes it is important to try harder, never hesitating to look to others for help. He will take others into consideration and is usually a team player. In other words, he works well with others and likes to offer a hand to friends and family members. For example, this person is always working for victory, but will call on others for help when concerns become too difficult to handle alone. The basketball player never gives up and is always focused on acquiring better coping strategies in order to progress through life as an emotionally healthy person.

Kendall is a forty-five year old recovering heroin addict. She is always focused for victory. She is thankful that she has a second chance at life with sobriety. She is caring and shows deep love for others, which is evident with all of the love she offers to fellow twelve step meeting members. She has learned to help herself by reflecting on inner needs and working through negative stressors as they arise. She feels secure in her recovery and is not afraid to ask others for help. She calls her sponsor almost daily and sometimes asks fellow group members for help. She is a team player and is also almost always available for others when they are in need. Talking through her concerns has helped Kendall evolve into a happy and healthy sober person.

Do you deal with life stressors as in a game of basketball?Describe._____
_____
_____
_____
_____
_____
_____
_____
_____
_____
_____

After reviewing all five games/approaches to dealing with life stressors, which sport best describes your way of dealing with stress? Elaborate._____

_____

_____

_____

_____

_____

There are numerous ways to combat stress and anxiety. You must decide which coping mechanism is best for your personality. As you become familiar with positive ways to handle stress, you will feel more peaceful and will want to face the world with confidence!

Talk therapy is one of the most valuable tools for coping with negative stressors. It is important to have a sober support system made up of people who understand and have experienced the disease of chemical dependency. They can relate to you and will offer helpful suggestions to you when you are having trouble thinking clearly. A sponsor is crucial in your recovery program. If you do not have a sponsor, it is not too late to attain one. Twelve step meetings are in every part of the world. Search on the internet or in your phone directory for a twelve step meeting. It is important to attend meetings in order to build a solid support system. You will be amazed at the support you will find from these groups. Twelve step meetings are a great place to vent frustrations and bottled feelings. You will feel more at peace with yourself, and you will greatly benefit from others wanting to listen to you. Twelve step meetings are filled with people who really care about you!

Do you have a sober support network? Who can you call when you need to talk?

_____

_____

_____

_____

_____

_____

_____

_____

_____

Do you have a sponsor? Have you developed friends as a result of involvement with twelve step meetings? Please list first names only in this book in order to protect anonymity.

_____

_____

_____

_____

_____

Artwork is an amazing expression of self. You are able to sketch any concerns or emotions with a variety of mediums. You can paint, use pencil, chalk, or clay when expressing your emotions through art. When you do not feel like talking about an issue, art is a healthy expression of emotion. The act of painting or drawing relaxes the mind and body and provides a way in which to let go of frustration and stress.

Aromatherapy is another soothing way to relieve stress. Lavender is a relaxing scent. Personally, I find the smell of honeysuckle to be relaxing. I suppose it is because I used to go on walks with my mom near a garden of honeysuckle as a small child. I have fond memories of those days and associate the scent of honeysuckle with those good times. You will find certain scents more relaxing than others, and it is all a matter of preference. You will often have happy memories tied to certain aromas. For example, you may find the scent of apple pie most relaxing and recall happy memories of your grandmother baking apple pie while you played with toys in her home many years ago.

Which scents do you find most relaxing? Are the aromas tied to any happy memories? Describe._____

_____

_____

_____

_____

_____

_____

_____

Relaxation and deep breathing techniques are effective strategies in which to effectively cope with stress. It is important to breathe through your diaphragm when practicing deep breathing. You must utilize all of the space in your lungs with cleansing breaths. You do not want to hyperventilate when practicing these exercises, so it is necessary that you breathe in through you nose and out through your mouth. With every inhale you should visually see your abdomen rise or expand. As you exhale, you will notice that your abdomen sinks inward. Visual imagery is a useful part of relaxation. You can close your eyes and focus on a beautiful scene while relaxing or practicing deep breathing techniques. It is amazing just how real your imagined scene will appear when you focus on sights, smells and sounds. I always picture the ocean with the waves crashing against the sand. I always concentrate on seagulls in the distance and the sounds of the waves. You will need to select a scene that is most relaxing to you.

Describe a scene that you would find relaxing. Describe any sights, aromas, or sounds in your imagined scenery._____

_____

_____

_____

_____

_____

_____

_____

_____

Music is a relaxing way to release stress. Music calms the mind and body. Some people release stress by singing loudly to music on the radio or while driving in the car. It is a wonderful alternative to an elevated harsh tone, which is common for some people who are suffering from elevated stress levels.

Pets are a marvelous way to cope with stress. Pets are shown to increase serotonin, the feel good chemicals in your brain. Pets are soft and cuddly and provide you with unconditional love.

Do you have a pet? Do you feel better after playing with your animal? Describe any stress release that you have noticed after interacting with a pet._____

_____

_____

_____

_____

_____

_____

_____

_____

Exercise is one of the most effective ways to alleviate the negative effects of stress and anxiety. Exercise helps to increase feel good chemicals, known as endorphins, in the body. Exercise helps to regulate blood sugar, blood pressure, and weight. Have you ever noticed how great you feel, both emotionally and physically, following an aerobic workout? Exercise helps the body relax and the mind to rejuvenate. If you are not fond of working out in a gym, there are other activities that are fun and may better suit your interests. Bicycling, hiking, swimming, walking, roller-skating, karate, basketball, softball, and playing tennis are wonderful activities to consider as forms of exercise. As I have mentioned previously in this book, it is important to consult with your physician before beginning any type of exercise. After you have received approval from your doctor, it is important to exercise at least three times per week for at least 20-30 minutes.

Do you exercise regularly?_____

_____

_____

_____

_____

_____

_____

_____

_____

Will you make a commitment to add a new activity or additional exercise to your lifestyle? Describe._____

_____

_____

_____

_____

_____

_____

_____

_____

_____

_____

Twenty simple ways to relax.

1. Receive a massage.
2. Surround yourself with soothing colors, such as pale blue and lavender. Paint your room with one of these relaxing colors.
3. Smile, even when you do not feel like smiling. The simple act of smiling will make you feel better.

4. Enjoy a hot bubble bath.

5. Enjoy your favorite comedy movie and laugh!

6. Start a new hobby that you enjoy.

7. Call or visit a friend.

8. Jump rope or play a game with a child.

9. Blow bubbles.

10. Take a walk in the rain.

11. Take a yoga class.

12. Visit the zoo or an amusement park.

13. Say a prayer.

14. Read a book that you find interesting.

15. Practice focusing on the positives in your life. Remember to say nice things to yourself. Pat yourself on the back when you do something well!

16. Eat healthy foods, which in turn will likely cause you to feel refreshed and energized.

17. Take a nap.

18. Practice stretching exercises during the day in order to relieve muscle tension.

19. Eat healthy crunchy snacks in order to help relieve jaw tension. Snacks such as apples and low-fat popcorn are excellent choices.

20. Practice deep breathing exercises several times a day.

Identify your favorite ways to relieve stress._____

_____

_____

_____

_____

_____

_____

_____

_____

_____

CHAPTER 7

THE IMPORTANCE OF HEALTHY RELATIONSHIPS AND EFFECTIVE COMMUNICATION

Involvement in healthy relationships and having effective communication skills are essential ingredients in the development of a sober person. Chances are you have probably been involved in some dangerous relationships during active addiction. Allow me to clearly define "dangerous relationships" in order to help you better understand. Dangerous relationships involve an alliance or a friendship between two persons that is emotionally damaging. Dangerous relationships will likely set you up for a relapse and will negatively impact psychological growth and development.

Dangerous relationships include relationships in which physical, emotional, and sexual abuse occurs. If you are being physically harmed, you need to contact a professional immediately for help. There are crisis centers available for immediate assistance. You may need to contact law enforcement in order to seek an immediate protection order. In no way should you ever stay around and tolerate any type of physical abuse. Emotional abuse can be equally as damaging to the psyche. Emotional abuse will deplete a person of positive self worth and may even escalate to violence. Sexual abuse can be equally as damaging. You should never have sex, unless you want to have sex. Never allow anyone to take advantage of you and your body. Codependent relationships are unhealthy and will hinder a person's search for a healthy sober identity. Relationships in which jealousy, resentments, and negativity are the main ingredients, are a recipe for disaster. Relationships in which one person drinks and drugs is considered dangerous for the other person. Think about how damaging it would be if a significant other or a close friend in your life used chemicals regularly. His behavior would negatively affect your thought processes and would likely encourage you to stumble. Just being around chemicals can stimulate the craving center in the brain. It is important for you to surround yourself with sober individuals who support your recovery efforts. These sober individuals in your life deserve your very best. You must invest time and energy into building healthy relationships.

Are you in a dangerous relationship currently? Describe why the relationship is considered to be dangerous. _____

_____

_____

_____

_____

_____

_____

    If your answer to the above stated question reflects an extremely dangerous situation in which violence exists, please contact a professional for help. Your life is worth saving. You must remove yourself from risky situations immediately!

    If you are being emotionally abused by a significant other, a friend, or a family member, you must set appropriate boundaries in order to prevent any further abuse. For example, if your wife is emotionally abusive and causes you to feel pain, it is important to communicate your feelings to your wife. If she calls you names and constantly criticizes you in front of others, it is time to tell her how you feel. She cannot continue to abuse you, because you will not allow it. You will decide to set boundaries, and simply will not tolerate abusive behavior. If you have voiced your concerns to your wife and she does not seem to hear you, it may be necessary to consult with a marriage counselor in order to resolve the issues. Examine the ways in which you have dealt with your wife's hurtful comments. Perhaps you respond to her with hateful and resentful words. When you respond to an angry wife with anger, it is not always productive. Keep in mind that anger fuels anger. Practice using "I Statements" as a healthy way to appropriately express your feelings to her. Be careful not to buy into the blame game because she will not hear you, and most likely will not change. You must communicate to your wife that you feel hurt when she uses those words or calls you certain names. If the behaviors continue, please consult with a professional because your emotional growth depends on it! You have made a commitment to discover your sober person, and you will be healthy and victorious in your venture!

Healthy Vs. Unhealthy Boundaries

UNHEALTHY

1. I share all of my innermost thoughts immediately after getting to know someone.
2. I fall in love too quickly.
3. I allow others to set my priorities.
4. I am sexual for someone even when I do not want to have sex.
5. I touch someone without asking or receiving signs that it is okay.

6. I do not notice when my boundaries have been invaded.
7. I accept food, gifts, touch, and sex when I am really not comfortable with the idea.
8. I allow others to constantly take from me.
9. I will violate my own values if you persuade me.
10. I allow others to direct the path of my life.
11. I expect other people to always fill my needs.
12. I allow others to physically, emotionally, and sexually abuse me.

HEALTHY

1. I allow relationships to grow before opening up.
2. I allow love to develop, without rushing things.
3. I understand and accept my own values.
4. I have sex when my partner and I desire the act.
5. I touch someone only after receiving signals that it is okay.
6. I do not allow others to be overly helpful or controlling.
7. I accept gifts only when I am comfortable.
8. I am aware of being taken advantage of and I do not allow it.
9. I will not depart from my own moral code.
10. I do not allow others to live my life for me.
11. I do not expect you to meet all of my needs.
12. I respect myself, and do not allow people to abuse me.

Describe unhealthy boundaries you are struggling with currently._____
_____
_____
_____
_____
_____
_____
_____
_____
_____
_____
_____

What specific actions or boundaries must you set in order to be healthy in your relationships?_____
_____
_____
_____

_____

_____

_____

_____

_____

_____

_____

_____

Boundaries are the dividing lines between you and anyone else in your life. The line represents both physical and emotional limits that others may not violate.

4 reasons why boundaries are necessary in relationships:

1. Personal boundaries are good for you. Setting boundaries raises self-esteem because you are sending yourself the message that you are worthy of self-care.
2. Boundaries are good for other people. They make others feel safe around you, and they demonstrate your limits.
3. Boundaries are a natural way of being. Everyone has his own individual boundary line. No two individuals share the very same exact boundary.
4. Having solid boundaries protects your body, mind, and spirit.

5 ways to establish solid boundaries

1. Become aware of your individual boundary lines. Establish some new boundaries that provide you with self-respect. Identify behaviors that you will no longer tolerate.
2. You must communicate to others your new boundaries. Communicate with an assertive style of communication, being careful not to blame or disrespect others.
3. Decide how you will communicate to others ways in which you would like to be treated. Perhaps you will need to have a meeting or write a letter in order to set boundaries with others.
4. Follow up with individuals regarding your relationship and any positive changes. When others are exhibiting behaviors that you have requested, thank them for honoring your new boundaries.
5. If persons do not respect your boundaries, you will need to provide consequences and remain consistent in your desire for positive change. You may even need to end a friendship if boundaries are emphatically denied. You must determine specific consequences and determine which relationships are worth the effort.

Codependency is an extremely common dynamic in chemically dependent families. Even after one chooses to work a recovery program, he or his family members will continue to exhibit unhealthy traits in relationships. Codependency is the act of assuming responsibility for another person's thoughts or feelings. Co-dependent relationships are not limited to chemically dependent families. Co-dependent relationships are seen in all walks of life. Perhaps you or someone close to you exhibits codependency traits.

The co-dependent person exhibits many of the following traits:

Good feelings come from another person liking me.
Good feelings about who I am are directly related to approval I receive from you.
I want to please you at all times.
I want to protect and take care of you.
I feel good when I solve your problems.
I feel happy when I make you feel good.
I do not worry about how I feel, because I am only concerned with how you feel.
My future goals are directly linked to you.
I put aside my values in order to please you.
I do not value my own opinion.
If you are happy, then I am happy.
If you are sad, then I am sad.
My fear of making you angry determines my actions.
I give of myself in order to feel safe in relationships.
I think I am attractive or smart only if you validate my appearance.
My circle of friends shrinks as I become involved with you.
I judge what I say, think, or do based on your standards.

Do you see any co-dependent traits in yourself?_____

_____

_____

_____

_____

_____

_____

_____

_____

Do you see co-dependent traits with any of your family members?_____

_____

_____

_____

_____

_____

_____

_____
_____
_____
_____
_____
_____

Do you have any friendships that reflect signs of co-dependent behaviors?_____
_____
_____
_____
_____
_____
_____
_____
_____
_____

Alcoholic families tend to have enablers who assume all responsibility for the chemically dependent person's thoughts, feelings, and actions. The enabler in the family tries to hide, help, and fix the chemically dependent person. In the meantime, the enabler as well as other family members become emotionally ill. Chemical dependency is a family disease, and therefore affects every person in the family unit. Communication in the alcoholic home becomes dishonest and shuts down. Discipline in an alcoholic home becomes irrational and inconsistent. Trust is a missing ingredient in an alcoholic home. Boundaries are often blurred in chemically dependent homes. It is important to relearn healthy communication styles in recovery in order to benefit from continued growth and emotional development.

There are four types of communication; however, only one type of healthy communication. The first type of communication is known as passive communication. This type of communication exists when a person avoids expressing inner thoughts and feelings. He holds everything in and usually suffers from feelings of low self-worth. This person does not have an opportunity to grow emotionally because he is not taking care of himself by expressing concerns and dealing with them. He feels as though he is not worth it! Passive communicators often speak softly and exhibit poor eye contact. They typically fail to assert themselves in most situations. Passive communicators are often very depressed and angry on the inside, as they allow little annoyances to build up over time. The danger of this type of communication is that issues are never addressed, which stunts any emotional development.

The second type of communication is aggressive communication. A person who exhibits aggressive communication is typically inappropriately loud and verbally attacks others. An aggressive communicator is dominating, controlling, and threatening to others. He tends to blame others, interrupts frequently, and uses "you statements". An example of a "you statement" is as follows: "You always make me angry!" No one person can always make you angry. An anger response is your individual reaction to something someone says or does. A person who responds with aggressive communication is often verbally or physically abusive, though not always. Aggressive communicators are almost always isolated from others and never deal with issues because their issues are always someone else's fault. This type of communication is extremely dangerous to recovery and healthy human development!

The third type of communication is known as passive—aggressive communication. This type of communicator appears to be passive on the outside, yet is really aggressive on the inside. This person acts out his anger in subtle and passive ways. For example, he may be extremely angry at his wife for selling his drums at a yard sale. Instead of confronting her about the action or expressing his feelings verbally, he smiles at her while planning his ploy. He, in turn, pawns a piece of her jewelry at a local pawn shop without her knowing. In the meantime, he mumbles angry words concerning his wife under his breath in a sarcastic tone. The passive-aggressive communicator often uses facial expressions that do not match how he feels. He uses secret sabotage to get even with another person. This person tends to release anger, yet never appropriately deals with important issues. He appears cooperative, but he really is not. This type of communication is not effective and hinders emotional development.

The fourth style of communication is assertive communication. This is a healthy and desired form of communication. This communicator clearly expresses his feelings and thoughts, and shows respect for other people. He feels connected to other people and stands up for his beliefs. He does not allow others to take advantage of him or to manipulate him in any way. He understands the importance of using "I Statements" when expressing thoughts. He is careful not to blame others and does not resort to name-calling or abuse. He maintains good posture and eye contact when expressing concerns. He uses a calm voice and does not yell to express thoughts or feelings. This type of communicator grows emotionally and is able to effectively deal with issues and concerns.

Which type of communication style do you usually exhibit?_____

_____

_____

_____

_____

_____

_____

_____

_____

_____

_____

_____

_____

_____

_____

_____

Identify positive changes that you need to consider in order to maximize optimum
growth and development in recovery._____

_____

_____

_____

_____

_____

_____

_____

_____

_____

_____

CHAPTER 8

HOW DO I PUT ALL OF THIS TOGETHER?

As you near the end of this book, you may be wondering how you will apply all of the helpful suggestions to your own life. Although it is no easy task, it is worth every effort that you must put forth in order to discover the new sober you! It is important to remember that it may take time and practice before you feel entirely comfortable with positive growth and change. Think about your using history for a moment. Ask yourself how many years you spent under the influence of mood altering chemicals. During that time period, you were not focused on healthy clear goals for your life. You were chasing your chemical, which became your first love above all else in your life. A drug may have robbed you of part of your life that you will never get back, but chemicals will not destroy your present life. You can be free and focused today, and that is what really matters most. I want to explore with you goals for today and for your future. Setting goals will help you to define where to go from here, and how to truly know yourself. Before you can identify individual goals, you must understand your values and priorities. Values and priorities play an important part in goal-setting.

MY VALUES ASSESSMENT

Please circle the things on the list that you strongly value.

After you circle the things that you value most, I want you to prioritize them. For example, start with the item most important to you and rank it a #1. Rank your top ten items. 1-10.

Religion
Your Children
Your Home
Material Possessions
Music
Art

Exercise
Integrity
Honesty
Helping Others
Health
God
Recreation
Hobbies
Happiness
Dance
Travel
Creativity
Security
Social Status
Physical Appearance
Personal Achievement
Wealth
Faith
Love
Education
Family
Solitude
Peace
Sports
Pets
Friends
Equality

Look closely at the values that you have identified as being important. Your values shape your priorities. Your priorities help to define who you are as a sober individual. Your priorities help you with goal setting, which is an important part of emotional development. Now I would like for you to evaluate your individual priorities. It is time to define personal goals.

Please list three personal goals that are easily attainable within the next 2 years. These need to be personal goals that you really desire to reach. Please do not set a goal that you do not believe is in your best interest or does not excite you. For example, if you selected sports as being of value for you, but you haven't had time to grow in that area, you will need to identify a short-term goal for that category. Let us pretend that you selected basketball as a value. It is important for you to evaluate short-term goals that will help you reach your long-term goal of being a professional basketball star. I will offer an example in order to make this concept clearer. I have a personal interest in karate and have a long-term goal of earning my black belt in two years. My short-term goal is that I will attend karate class at least two days a week and will practice two days a week on my own time. If I work toward the objectives or actions that I have identified, I should be able to reach my goal. If I neglect to put forth effort, I will most likely fail at reaching my goal.

Now I would like you to identify an attainable long-term goal for your future.

_____

_____

_____

Now you must identify three short-term goals or action steps necessary in order to meet your long-term goal.

1._____

_____

2._____

_____

3._____

_____

_____

Congratulations! You are on your way to beginning a new sober lifestyle, and you are simply wonderful for not giving up. During active addiction, you would have given up easily in search of the quick fix. As a sober person, you now understand that a quick fix does not exist. You are working diligently for positive change and you will reap the rewards from having a sober lifestyle. The search for your sober self has already been an adventure and will continue to be exciting as you make progress toward making positive changes in your life. It will be extremely important for you to measure progress toward working through identity issues and discovering your sober self. I am sure you are wondering how you might measure progress for a concept that seems so complex. It is really much simpler than it sounds. You will continue to set goals for yourself in order to evaluate your success. You will practice handling emotions in effective ways. If you mess up and react to a stressor or an emotion in a negative way, do not become discouraged and give up. It will take time for you to choose correct actions in dealing with specific events and emotions. It is important not to allow a wrong choice to set you back into a cycle of defeat or guilt. Simply hold your head up high and tell yourself that you are worthy and can work for a victory! On a daily basis you must take a personal inventory in order to evaluate whether or not you have buried feelings that particular day. If you have, you must set short-term goals that will help you to stay focused and aid you as you explore any hidden feelings. You may need to start a goal diary in order for you to keep track of any positive changes that must be addressed. A spiral notebook or notepad will serve well as a goal diary. Record thoughts, feelings, actions, accomplishments, and potential areas for improvement on a daily basis.

MY DAILY GOAL DIARY

SUNDAY: TODAY'S DATE

ACTIVITIES I WAS INVOLVED IN TODAY INCLUDE:

HOW DID I FEEL OVERALL TODAY?

WHAT DID I ACCOMPLISH TODAY?

DID ANY OF MY ACTIONS OR THOUGHTS INTERFERE WITH MY EMOTIONAL GROWTH TODAY?

HOW WILL I CREATE POSITIVE CHANGE FOR ANY INCORRECT CHOICES OR SETBACKS?

MONDAY/ TODAY'S DATE

ACTIVITIES I WAS INVOLVED IN TODAY INCLUDE:

HOW DID I FEEL OVERALL TODAY?

WHAT DID I ACCOMPLISH TODAY?

DID ANY OF MY ACTIONS OR THOUGHTS INTERFERE WITH MY EMOTIONAL GROWTH TODAY?

HOW WILL I CREATE POSITIVE CHANGE FOR ANY INCORRECT CHOICES OR SETBACKS?

TUESDAY/TODAY'S DATE

ACTIVITIES I WAS INVOLVED IN TODAY INCLUDE:

HOW DID I FEEL OVERALL TODAY?

WHAT DID I ACCOMPLISH TODAY?

DID ANY OF MY ACTIONS OR THOUGHTS INTERFERE WITH MY EMOTIONAL GROWTH TODAY?

HOW WILL I CREATE POSITIVE CHANGE FOR ANY INCORRECT CHOICES OR SETBACKS?

WEDNESDAY/TODAY'S DATE

ACTIVITIES I WAS INVOLVED IN TODAY INCLUDE:

HOW DID I FEEL OVERALL TODAY?

WHAT DID I ACCOMPLISH TODAY?

DID ANY OF MY ACTIONS OR THOUGHTS INTERFERE WITH MY EMOTIONAL GROWTH TODAY?

HOW WILL I CREATE POSITIVE CHANGE FOR ANY INCORRECT CHOICES OR SETBACKS?

THURSDAY/TODAY'S DATE

ACTIVITIES I WAS INVOLVED IN TODAY INCLUDE:

HOW DID I FEEL OVERALL TODAY?

WHAT DID I ACCOMPLISH TODAY?

DID ANY OF MY ACTIONS OR THOUGHTS INTERFERE WITH MY EMOTIONAL GROWTH TODAY?

HOW WILL I CREATE POSITIVE CHANGE FOR ANY INCORRECT CHOICES OR SETBACKS?

FRIDAY/TODAY'S DATE

ACTIVITIES I WAS INVOLVED IN TODAY INCLUDE:

HOW DID I FEEL OVERALL TODAY?

WHAT DID I ACCOMPLISH TODAY?

DID ANY OF MY ACTIONS OR THOUGHTS INTERFERE WITH MY EMOTIONAL GROWTH TODAY?

HOW WILL I CREATE POSITIVE CHANGE FOR ANY INCORRECT CHOICES OR SETBACKS?

SATURDAY/TODAY'S DATE

ACTIVITIES I WAS INVOLVED IN TODAY INCLUDE:

HOW DID I FEEL OVERALL TODAY?

WHAT DID I ACCOMPLISH TODAY?

DID ANY OF MY ACTIONS OR THOUGHTS INTERFERE WITH MY EMOTIONAL GROWTH TODAY?

HOW WILL I CREATE POSITIVE CHANGE FOR ANY INCORRECT CHOICES OR SETBACKS?

One of the best ways to measure success toward meeting personal goals is to write yourself a letter. This letter will be very important to your future, so I hope that you choose to commit to this task. You will focus on self-affirmations and character strengths. Remind yourself how amazing you really are. Congratulate yourself regarding your sober lifestyle, and make a point to remember all of your many blessings in sobriety. Focusing on yourself in such a positive light may feel awkward, yet it is an important activity concerning self-discovery and emotional growth. Remember that this letter is to yourself, so you are not bragging to the world. In this letter you will also need to set personal goals that will be met in a twelve month time period. For example, if you have a positive goal of attending college next fall, you will identify actions necessary to meet the goal. You will need to do research on colleges in the area or make a decision to relocate to another area. You may need to apply for grants or scholarships. Perhaps one of your goals will be to become more honest about feelings. You may need to write in a feelings journal every day. Maybe you will decide to phone your sponsor on a daily basis in order to process emotions. It may be necessary for you to seek counsel from an experienced therapist who will help you with emotional management. Perhaps you desire to start a new hobby, such as art. It would be beneficial to save money in order to purchase art supplies. It may be necessary to take a few art classes.

Exactly one year from the day you write the letter to yourself, you will review the letter. Evaluate whether you were able to meet all of your goals. Ask yourself if you have been practicing correct thinking. Are you continuing to grow by allowing feelings to flow? Are you effectively coping with feelings? Has your life improved over the last year? One year later, if you answer yes to these questions, your self-esteem will have likely improved and you will be content with personal growth. If you find that you were unable to stay focused and did not meet identified goals, it will present an opportunity for you to become refocused and will help redirect your sober path. You will have an opportunity to set new goals and to reflect on improving life circumstances through right thinking and behavior. If you make a commitment to follow through with the letter writing activity, it will be a win-win situation, and you will surely shine as a sober and special individual.

DEAR _____

_____

_____

_____

_____

_____

_____

_____

_____

   Now that you have written your letter, you will want to make a note of today's date. You will need to think of a way to remember the importance of reviewing your letter exactly one year from today. Perhaps you will associate today with the birthday or anniversary of a friend or a grandparent. Maybe you will need to write a note and post it where you will see the reminder one year from today. After you evaluate your letter next year, you may need to read the book again as a way to refresh your mind concerning all of the important concepts.

   I want to thank you for taking time to fully immerse yourself in this book and for your desire to truly understand yourself as a sober person. You are an outstanding person who is dedicated to positive change and sobriety. I wish for you many days of happy sober living and a life filled with peace.